MOMENTS IN SPORTS

from the Associated Press

GALLERY BOOKS
An imprint of W.H. Smith Publishers Inc.
112 Madison Avenue
New York, New York 10016

ISBN 0-8317-6085-0

Project Director: Dan Perkes
Photo Editor: Brian Horton
Photo Research: Marilyn E. Dillon
Written by Norm Goldstein
Design by CBG Graphics

Prepared and Produced by
Wieser & Wieser, Inc. 80 Madison Avenue
New York, New York, 10016

Photos by the staff and member newspaper photographers
of the Associated Press

Moments in sports.

   1. Sports—History—Pictorial works.   I. Associated
Press.
GV571.M66   1985   796'.09   85-14320
ISBN 0-8317-6085-0

Printed in Hong Kong

Published by Gallery Books
A Division of W. H. Smith Publishers Inc.
112 Madison Avenue
New York, New York 10016

INTRODUCTION

The best sports writers are artists, using words to draw the dramas they see. They sketch the scene with detail and color it with emotion, and the readers can see it in their minds.

Yet, no word picture, no matter how precise or poignant, is complete without the real picture that lets readers see it with their own eyes.

Lou Gehrig wiping a tear in his farewell at Yankee Stadium.

Henry Aaron watching the flight of his 715th home run.

Yogi Berra jumping into Don Larsen's arms after the only perfect game in World Series history.

Muhammad Ali shaking his fist in exultation over a fallen Sonny Liston.

Swede Savage sitting in a pool of fire in the middle of the Indianapolis Motor Speedway.

Y.A. Tittle, battered and bleeding, on his knees after being hit hard while passing.

Doug Flutie's last-second, desperation pass heading for its rendezvous with college football legend.

Roger Bannister breaking the tape as the first person ever to run the mile in less than 4 minutes.

Mary Decker lying in agony after tripping over Zola Budd in the Los Angeles Olympics.

Flag-waving members of the U.S. hockey team after winning the gold medal at the Lake Placid Olympics.

They run the gamut, from glee to sadness, celebration to frustration, success to failure.

But these are only words. This is a book of photos. They speak for themselves.

DARRELL CHRISTIAN
Sports Editor
The Associated Press

EARLY DAYS

Citius, altius, fortius.
Faster, higher, braver.
The motto of the Olympic Games.
The Winter Games . . . powdery snow . . .
blue-white ice . . . spills, thrills and chills.
The Summer Games . . . early memories of
Jesse Owens . . . Paavo Nurmi, the Flying Finn.
The Golden Age of Sports . . . Ruth and
Gehrig . . . Tunney and Dempsey . . . Man O'War
. . . Joe Louis . . . Red Grange . . . Knute
Rockne.

Track star Jesse Owens astonished the world at the
Berlin Olympics in 1936.

4

World Champion

The athlete who became known as the fastest man on earth won four gold medals—for the long jump, the 100-meter run, the 200-meter run, and as a member of the 400-meter relay team.

   His victories also became a symbol of freedom in the face of Nazi Germany.

The Rock

Knute Rockne was one of the greatest college football coaches. In the 13 years he coached at Notre Dame, the Irish won 6 national championships, beat Stanford in the 1925 Rose Bowl, and had 5 unbeaten and untied seasons. His lifetime winning record between 1918 and 1931 was 105–12–5.

The Norwegian-born Rockne himself played football for Notre Dame in 1913.

He was well known for his football strategy, which stressed the forward pass at a time when most teams kept the ball on the ground, and for fast, deceptive plays. He was noted, too, for his insistence on good sportsmanship.

He was still coaching in 1931 when he died in a plane crash.

The lineup before the start 500 mile race - May 30, 1912 Indianapolis Motor Speedway. C.F. Bretzman Indpls. Official Photographer

Indianapolis

Here's what the Indianapolis 500 race course looked like in 1912.
    Joe Dawson won the 500 that year with a speed of 78.72 m.p.h.
    Drivers today go at twice that speed.

Flying Finn

Paavo Nurmi, the famous "Flying Finn," is shown winning the 5,000-meter race in Paris in 1924.

Twenty-eight years later, he was given the honor of lighting the Olympic flame to open the games in his home city of Helsinki. He was 55 years old.

Nurmi set 19 world records in the 1920s.

Sultan of Swat

Big, lovable George Herman "Babe" Ruth, the "Sultan of Swat," was more than a baseball star. He was a symbol, the personification of all that was great and spectacular in the game.

He revolutionized the sport, turning baseball from a pitcher's stronghold to a batter's paradise.

Nobody then, before, and for a long time after, could hit the home run the way he could and please the crowd with the long ball.

He hit 714 home runs in his career, including 60 in the 1927 season. He had a slugging percentage of .847 in one season and a lifetime slugging average of .690. His lifetime batting average was .342.

"Shucks," he once said, "I could have hit a .600 lifetime average easy. But I would have to had hit singles. People were paying to see me hit home runs."

The Best and the Brightest

It was "the Called Shot."

In the fifth inning of the third game of the 1932 World Series with the Chicago Cubs, New York Yankee great Babe Ruth was being heckled when he came to bat against Charley Root. Root fired two quick strikes—called in unison by Ruth and umpire Roy Van Graflan.

Then Ruth stepped out, made a "it-only-takes-one-to-hit-it" gesture toward the distant right field bleachers—and belted the next one out there.

The Cubs were silent as the Babe came around and accepted the congratulations of another Yankee great, Lou Gehrig, who was up next.

Even Van Graflan smiled.

The Yankees swept the Series in four.

Two of the greatest ever to play the game, Gehrig and Ruth were given memorable and emotional farewells on separate occasions at Yankee Stadium, "the House that Ruth Built."

Gehrig, the "Iron Man," who set the record of 2,130 consecutive games playing first base for the Yankees between June 1, 1925, and April 30, 1939, was paid tribute by some 60,000 people on July 4, 1939.

Tears were in his eyes as he said good-bye to his beloved game: "I have been given a bad break, but I have an awful lot to live for."

He died in June 1941, of a debilitating muscle disease that later became known as "Lou Gehrig's disease."

Babe Ruth's number, 3, was retired on June 13, 1948, when fans and players commemorated the 25th anniversary of Yankee Stadium. In a raspy voice, the ailing Sultan of Swat said farewell to the misty-eyed gathering. He died of cancer two months later.

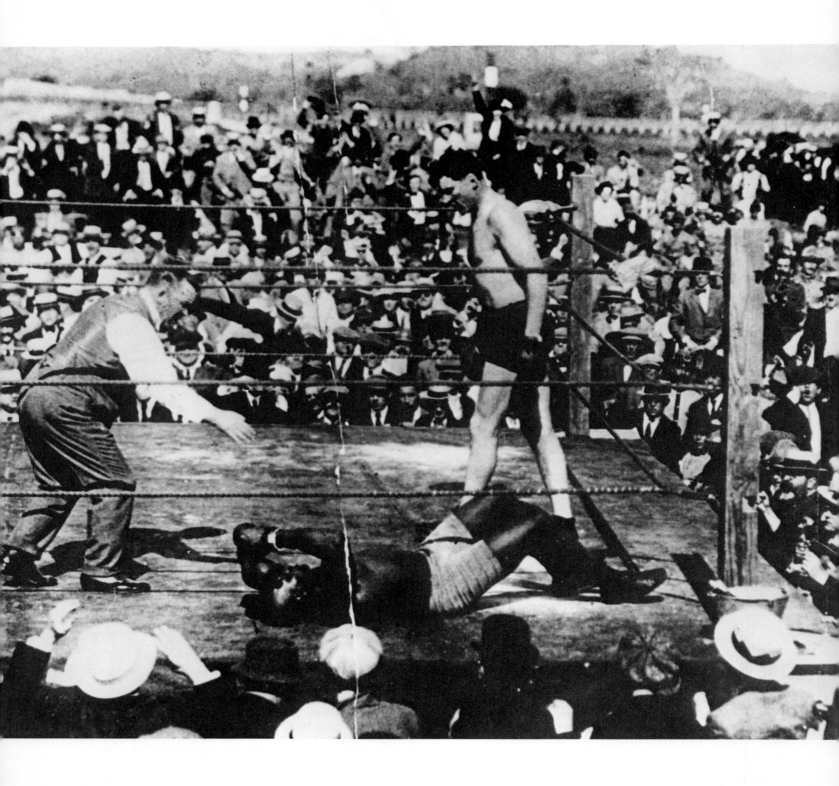

Hot and Heavy

April 5, 1915. A scorching day in the sun in Havana, Cuba. Surely no day for an outdoor boxing match, and certainly not a scheduled 45 rounds.

But that was the day Jess Willard knocked out champion Jack Johnson in the 26th round to take the heavyweight title.

The photo of the knockout showing Johnson on his back, apparently shading the sun from his eyes, became one of boxing's most famous. Johnson's detractors claimed it showed that he quit.

The Long Count

Heavyweight champion Gene Tunney was down and was being counted out in the seventh round of this rematch with Jack Dempsey, the "Manassa Mauler," in Chicago in 1927.

But the count never got to 10.

Referee Dave Barry didn't start the count until Dempsey went to a neutral corner. Only then did he start counting. Tunney was on the floor at least 14 seconds in a bout that became known as the "Long Count."

Tunney got up, knocked Dempsey down in the next round, and won a 10-round decision.

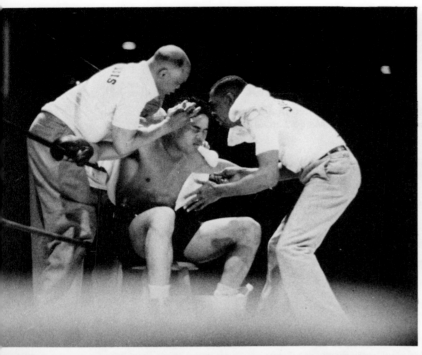

16

Brown Bomber

Joe Louis, the popular "Brown Bomber," defended his heavyweight championship title a record 25 times.

The most memorable were his bouts with Max Schmeling.

In June 1936, Schmeling had knocked Louis out in the 12th round, the first time he'd ever been KO'd.

The rematch was held in Yankee Stadium on June 22, 1938, before a crowd of 70,000. Adding to the drama of the rematch were the facts that Schmeling was German, it was 1938, and Adolf Hitler was in power.

This one ended in two minutes and four seconds of the first round. Louis had knocked Schmeling down three times, and referee Arthur Donovan called a halt. On the third knockdown, Schmeling landed on all fours, and a towel was thrown in from his corner. The referee hurled it back. Then he looked at Schmeling, heard the timekeeper reach a count of eight, and stopped the fight.

Louis held his title from 1937 to 1949.

He tried a comeback in 1951, but Rocky Marciano knocked any such thoughts out of him in the eighth round.

Wrong Way Run

In the 1929 Rose Bowl, California center Roy Riegels earned a special place in the history of football. The wrong way.

Georgia Tech had fumbled on its own 20-yard line, and Riegels recovered. He turned and ran 65 yards. In the wrong direction.

Teammate Benny Lom caught him at the one-yard line, but it wasn't enough. California was forced to punt, the ball was partially blocked, and Georgia Tech got a safety. They won 8–7.

Galloping Ghost

Harold "Red" Grange, a.k.a. the "Galloping Ghost."

He earned the sobriquet when he scored five touchdowns the first five times he carried the ball for the University of Illinois against Michigan in 1924. He scored 31 touchdowns in three seasons of college ball.

Grange also played pro football with the old New York Yankees and the Chicago Bears.

First Nighter

Quick: when and where was the first night baseball game in the major leagues?
  Right. Crosley Field, Cincinnati, May 24, 1935, the Reds against the Philadelphia Phillies.

Night Ball

It was the first night baseball game in the East, and Johnny Vander Meer made it a memorable one.

The Cincinnati Reds pitcher threw a 6–0 no-hitter against the Brooklyn Dodgers that night, June 15, 1938, at Brooklyn's Ebbets Field.

Night or day didn't make much difference to Vander Meer. He had pitched another no-hitter in his previous outing four days earlier.

"The Mostest Hoss"

One of the most popular—and spectacular—horses in racing history was Man O'War, once described as "a roaring red comet."

He won 20 races in 21 tries, each victory by a sizable margin. His only defeat,—in 1919, when he was a two-year-old,—was to a horse named, incredibly, Upset. With Willie Knapp driving, Upset (No. 4) beat out No. 1 in the Sanford Stakes at Saratoga.

Man O'War quickly avenged the defeat. Here, he wins the 1920 Travers Stakes ahead of No. 3 (John P. Grier), and Upset (No. 2). Upset lost five decisions to the champion after his one win.

In his time, Man O'War set three world records, two U.S. marks, and three track records.

Visitors filed past his casket in the Lexington, Kentucky, stall where he spent his declining years before he died in 1947.

FORTIES

The Sport of Kings . . . the glamorous Kentucky Derby . . . the Triple Crown.
   In the 1940s, the likes of Citation . . . Assault . . . Whirlaway . . . Count Fleet.
   The decade of DiMaggio and Williams . . . Bevens' near no-hitter . . . Mickey Owen's infamous passed ball . . . Gionfriddo's catch.

The Triple Crown of horse racing means winning three major races: the Kentucky Derby, the Preakness, the Belmont Stakes.
   Only 11 horses have done it.
   One was Citation.

Speeding Citation

Ridden by Eddie Arcaro, who piloted five Derby winners in his career, Citation took the Triple Crown in 1948. In the last and longest of the three races, the Belmont, he won by eight lengths.

In these photos, Citation (No. 1) is shown at the finish ahead of Kitchen (No. 2) in the 1948 Ground Hog at Hialeah, February 2, 1948; crossing the finish line 3½ lengths ahead of stablemate Coaltown (1a) at the Kentucky Derby in May 1948; and racing through the stretch run to win the Belmont Stakes by six lengths the same Triple Crown year.

Joltin' Joe

Joe DiMaggio, one of the greatest outfielders in baseball history, was one of three brothers to play the game professionally (with Vince and Dom).

Joltin' Joe played with the New York Yankees from 1936 to 1951 and finished with a lifetime batting average of .325, having played in 10 World Series and 11 All-Star games. He was the American League's Most Valuable Player in 1939, 1941, and 1947.

His consecutive-game hitting record of 56, set in 1941, still stands.

Here, in his first appearance in Washington, D.C., on April 30, 1938, DiMaggio singled his first time up and scored when Bill Dickey doubled against the Senators.

Splendid Splinter

For the pure art—nay, science—of hitting, there was none better than the "Splendid Splinter," Boston Red Sox Ted Williams.

He batted .406 in 1941. No one has hit .400 since.

He won six American League batting titles and retired in 1960 with a lifetime average of .344.

He managed the Washington Senators (now the Texas Rangers) from 1969 to 1972 and later served as minor league batting coach in the Red Sox farm system.

He wrote the book on batting.

Almost . . .

Floyd "Bill" Bevens could have told you how difficult it is to pitch a no-hitter in a World Series game.

He had one going for the New York Yankees in the fourth game against the Brooklyn Dodgers in 1947. It was the bottom of the ninth inning, the Yankees ahead 2–1.

Bevens got Bruce Edwards to fly to left. Then he walked Carl Furillo. Al Gionfriddo came in to run for Furillo. Then Bevens got Spider Jorgensen to pop out. It was one out to go.

Pete Reiser pinch-hit for Dodger relief pitcher Hugh Casey. Gionfriddo stole second, and Reiser was walked intentionally. Still one out to go. Still no hits.

Cookie Lavagetto was sent in to hit for Eddie Stanky, as Eddie Miksis ran for Reiser.

On an 0–1 pitch, Lavagetto hit a line drive off the right field wall, and both Gionfriddo and Miksis scored. End of no-hitter. End of game. Dodgers win, 3–2.

That's Bevens and Joe DiMaggio walking down the clubhouse runway after the game.

In 1952, when the Dodgers and Cincinnati played an exhibition game in Florida, Bevens (who had been traded to the Reds) was able to joke about it with Lavagetto.

But only Lavagetto laughed in 1947.

Catch This Catch

It was the sixth game of the 1947 World Series. Once again, the opponents were the New York Yankees and the Brooklyn Dodgers.

The Yankees led the Series, three games to two. Brooklyn took the early lead with four runs, but the Yankees came back and went ahead, 5–4. Then, the Dodgers scored four in the sixth and led, 8–5.

In the bottom of the sixth, little Al Gionfriddo, a seldom-used utility man, went out to left field as a defensive substitute. With two out and two runners on, Joe DiMaggio, the "Yankee Clipper," came up, knowing full well that a home run would tie it.

DiMaggio hit Joe Hatten's pitch solidly. Gionfriddo turned his back to the plate and started to run. And run. When he ran out of room to run, he stretched and leapt at the bullpen fence. And caught it.

It was one of the great catches of World Series history.

But the Yankees came back the next day to win the seventh and deciding contest.

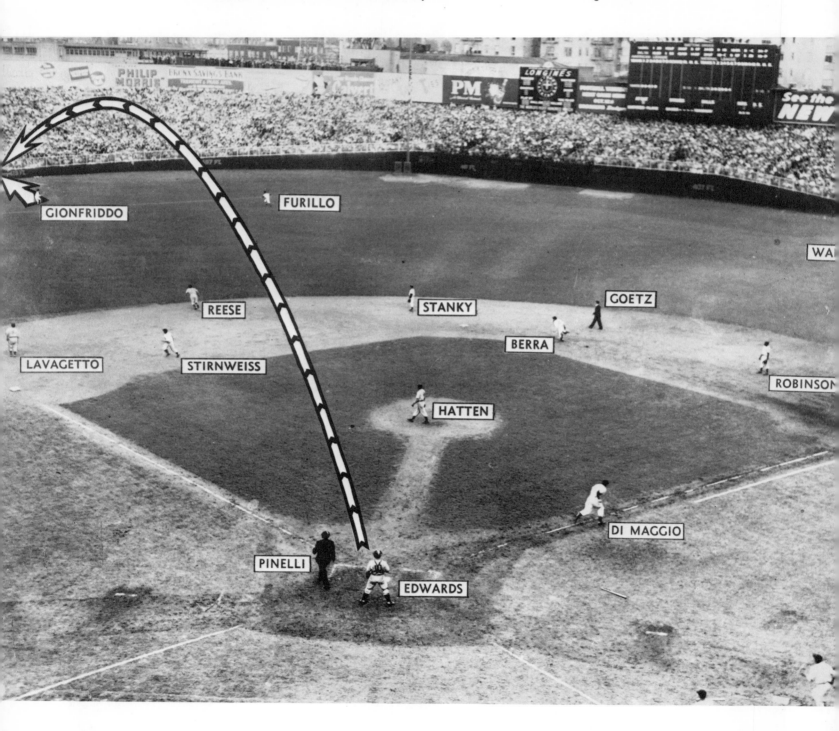

It Ain't Over Until It's Over

Nothing exemplified the theory that no game is over until the final out the way this game did.

And no team probably ever suffered a more painful World Series loss than the Brooklyn Dodgers did this October 5, 1941.

Dodger relief pitcher Hugh Casey was protecting a 4–3 lead against the New York Yankees with two out in the ninth inning of the fourth game. He struck out Tommy Henrich. It should have been over.

But Dodger catcher Mickey Owen dropped the third strike, and Henrich made it to first. Given a second chance, the Yankees scored four more runs to win it, 7–4. Here, Joe DiMaggio slides home safely with the Yankees' fifth run.

Jackie Robinson

Jackie Robinson, a dazzling, base-stealing, all-around baseball player, helped the Brooklyn Dodgers to six National League pennants—and their only World Series win, in 1955. He played 10 major league seasons and batted .311.

And he did it all with the added pressure of being the first black player in modern American major league baseball.

Here, Robinson loses his hat but steals home safely in a game against the Philadelphia Phillies, July 2, 1950. Catcher Andy Seminick makes the late tag as Dodger batter Gil Hodges watches.

At right, Robinson tags out New York Yankee Yogi Berra to start a third inning double play in the sixth game of the Yankees-Dodgers World Series in 1955.

FIFTIES

Baseball in the 1950s: great games . . . great names.

Bobby Thomson's dramatic playoff home run . . . "The Catch" by Willie Mays . . . Don Larsen's perfect World Series . . . The Yankees' six straight championships . . . and the Brooklyn Dodgers' first and only title.

Yogi Berra . . . Casey Stengel . . . Sandy Amoros . . . Jackie Robinson . . . midget Eddie Gaedel.

The memorable Colts-Giants overtime NFL Championship game. . . .

The era of Bob Cousy . . . the four-minute mile . . . Emil Zatopek . . . Ben Hogan.

There was no joy in Brooklyn.

Bobby Thomson did not strike out.

Instead, Thomson hit a two-out, three-run home run off Brooklyn Dodger relief pitcher Ralph Branca (No. 13), and the New York Giants won the 1951 National League pennant.

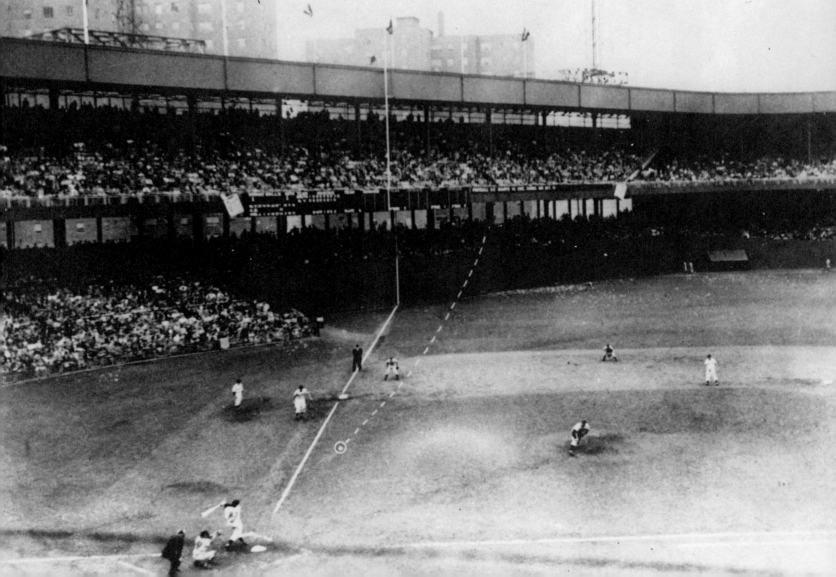

Miracle At Coogan's Bluff

"The Giants win the pennant: The Giants win the pennant! The Giants win the pennant!" Radio announcer Russ Hodges kept repeating what was almost unbelievable.

The Giants were behind 13½ games in August and came back to force the Dodgers into a 3-game playoff. The Dodgers were ahead, 4–2, in the ninth inning of the final game, when Thomson came up to hit with two men on. It was the home run "heard 'round the world." (Willie Mays was on deck, but . . . .)

What Might Have Been . . .

Cal Abrams of the Brooklyn Dodgers is tagged out by Philadelphia Phillies catcher Stan Lopata in the ninth inning of a game at Ebbets Field on October 1, 1950.

Abrams tried to make it home from second base after Duke Snider had singled, but center fielder Richie Ashburn threw him out.

If Abrams had scored, it would have given the Dodgers the game—and a tie for the National League pennant.

But the Phils won and clinched their first pennant in 35 years.

Squeeze Play

A ninth-inning squeeze bunt off the bat of New York Yankee Phil Rizzuto brought Joe DiMaggio home with the winning run in a game against the Cleveland Indians at Yankee Stadium, September 17, 1951.

Cleveland catcher Jim Hegan, already conceding defeat, starts for the dugout as DiMaggio scores before pitcher Bob Lemon can try for a play at the plate.

Yogi

The World Series just doesn't seem the same without Yogi Berra.

He spent 21 seasons in a postseason championship, either as player, coach, or manager, beginning in 1947 when he played with the New York Yankees against the Brooklyn Dodgers. In that Series, he hit a pinch-hit homer in his first time at bat.

His records for World Series—games, 75; at bats, 259; hits, 71; singles, 49; and consecutive errorless games, 30—may never be matched. He was the catcher for the Yankees in the only perfect no-hit World Series game, Don Larsen's, in 1956.

The colorful catcher also managed the Yankees and the New York Mets.

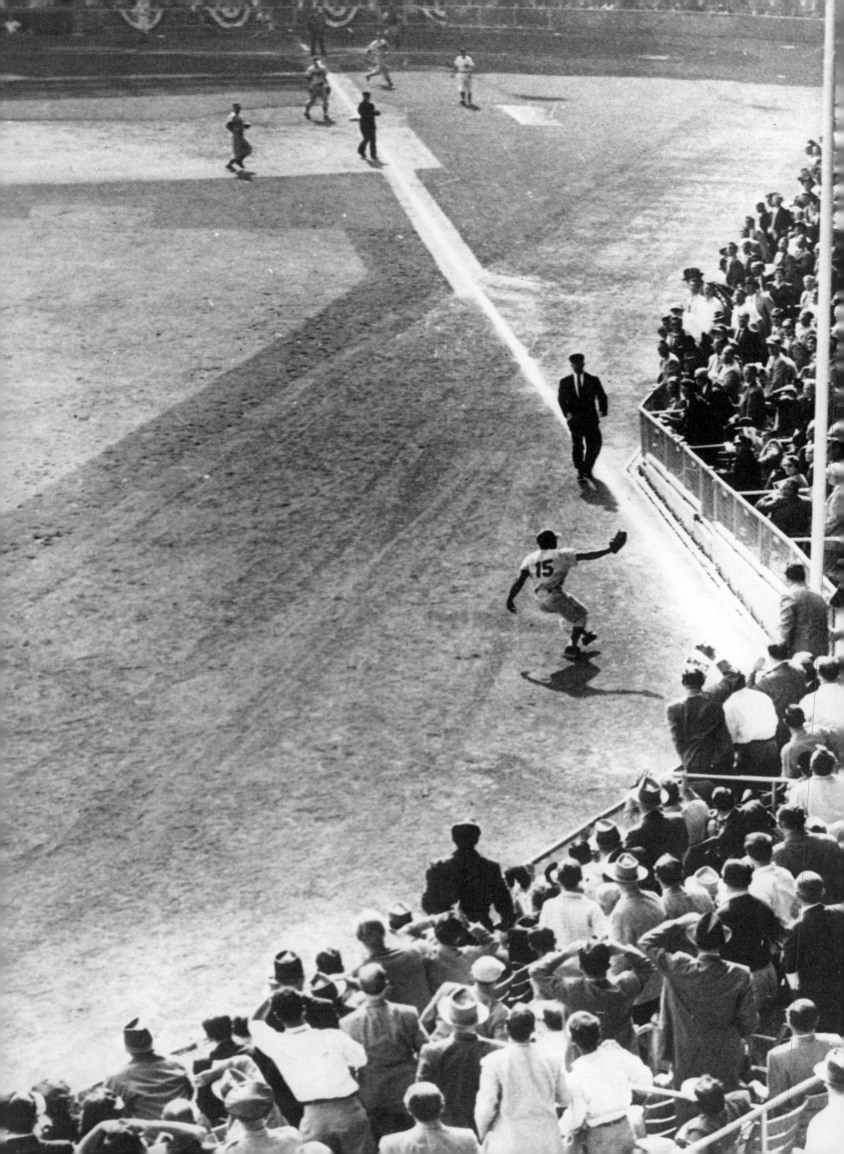

Handy Sandy

Somehow, the spectacular comes out in World Series games.

In this one in Yankee Stadium in 1955, the hero was Sandy Amoros, left fielder for the Brooklyn Dodgers.

With two men on base in the sixth inning of the final game, Yogi Berra hit what looked like a game-tying shot down the left field line. The Yankees were behind 2–0 at the time, and there were no outs.

But Amoros made the memorable grab and threw back quickly to double up Gil McDougald at first.

The Dodgers went on to win it—their first-ever World Series victory after seven losses.

The Flying Dutchwoman

In action—in the women's 100-meter run in the 1952 Olympics and in the broad jump at a meet in Amsterdam in 1956—is Fanny Blankers-Koen, the "Flying Dutchwoman."

She finished her 22-year athletic career with the 17-foot 2-inch broad jump, her farewell performance.

The mother of two had won four gold medals at the 1948 Olympics in London and had been champion of Holland in the 100-meter, 200-meter, high jump, broad jump, shot-put, and pentathlon events.

Czech Another Record

One of track and field's great long-distance runners, Emil Zatopek of Czechoslovakia broke the 5,000-meter Olympic record at Helsinki, Finland, in 1952. Behind him were Alain Mimoun of France and Herbert Schade of Germany.

Zatopek's time of 14:06.6 has since been topped.

The Czech set 18 world records in his career and won 4 gold medals at the Olympics, from 5,000 meters through the marathon.

Historic Mile

Time flies.

It was in 1954, on the sixth of May, that Roger Bannister became the first man to run the mile in less than four minutes.

Running for the Amateur Athletic Association against Oxford University at Oxford, the British athlete hit the tape with a time of 3:59.4.

Today, sub-four-minute miles seem almost commonplace; more than 12 seconds have been cut from Bannister's mark.

Say, Hey!

In the old New York Polo Grounds, there was plenty of room in center field. Just right for one of the greatest outfielders ever to play baseball.

This was one of the most famous catches of all time.

Willie Mays ran, with his back to the plate, to reach out and grab a 450-foot shot off the bat of Vic Wertz in the eighth inning of the World Series opener against the Cleveland Indians in 1954. He made the catch with two runners on base and may have made the difference in the game, as the Giants won it, 5–2, on a 10th-inning pinch-hit home run by Dusty Rhodes.

Fellow players complimented him: "He made the hard ones look easy."

Mays said of "the Catch," "I don't compare them. I just catch them."

Throughout his career, Mays electrified crowds with his fielding, explosive hitting and daring base running. He hit 660 home runs in his career and was the National League's Most Valuable Player in 1954, when he won the league batting title, and in 1965.

A Perfect Day

Ah, perfection, the thing that dreams are made of.

Flawlessness.

In baseball, 27 up, 27 down. No mistakes. No runs, no hits, no errors, no walks, no one gets to first base but the opposition coach.

Unique in a World Series.

Don Larsen, October 8, 1956. A no-hitter. A perfect no-hitter.

New York Yankee catcher Yogi Berra was the first to demonstrate the elation as he leapt on Larsen after the last Brooklyn Dodger had come up for his shot and walked away like all the others. Out.

Dale Mitchell, a pinch hitter, was the 27th batter to face the New York Yankee pitcher in that fifth game. He watched the third strike go by and heard the deafening roar of the Yankee Stadium crowd admiring a spectacular achievement in baseball history.

Oh, yes, the Yankees won, 2–0.

A Short Story

It's not Little League.

It's professional baseball, August 1951.

Ed Gaedel, 26-year-old Chicago stuntman, was sent up to bat as a pinch-hitter for Bill Veeck's St. Louis Browns in the first inning of the second game of a doubleheader against the Detroit Tigers.

Guess what? Gaedel walked on four high pitches to catcher Bob Swift.

Jim Delsing was sent in to run for Gaedel, who pinch-hit for outfielder Frank Saucier.

Umpire Ed Hurley had examined Gaedel's contract before allowing him to bat. His name had appeared on the Brown's roster for the previous few days.

Baseball rules were later changed. It couldn't happen again.

Casey Stengel

Charles Dillon Stengel, the man known as "Casey" for nearly six decades of professional baseball, managed the New York Yankees to amazing triumphs and finished his career managing the New York Mets to amazingly popular losses.

While manager of the Yankees between 1949 and 1960, his team won 10 pennants and 7 world championships. As the first manager of the New York Mets, his team finished last in each of his four seasons with them.

Through it all, he was one of the most popular and theatrical characters in all of baseball. Known as the "Professor," he earned a dubious reputation for his monologues and storytelling in "Stengelese," a gobbledygook doubletalk that defied analysis.

54

Master Hogan

The classic swing and determined style of Ben Hogan was evident over the years.

The Texas-born golfer had overcome a nearly fatal accident to become one of the best players in the world.

A year after he won the 1948 U.S. Open, he was in an automobile accident, and doctors said he might never walk again. He not only walked, he won the U.S. Open in 1950, the Open and the Masters in 1951, and the Open, Masters, and British Open in 1953.

This May 30, 1971, photograph shows Hogan taking his last shot in professional golf competition, a tee shot on the 12th hole at a tournament in Houston. He sent his caddy after the ball and took the cart to the clubhouse.

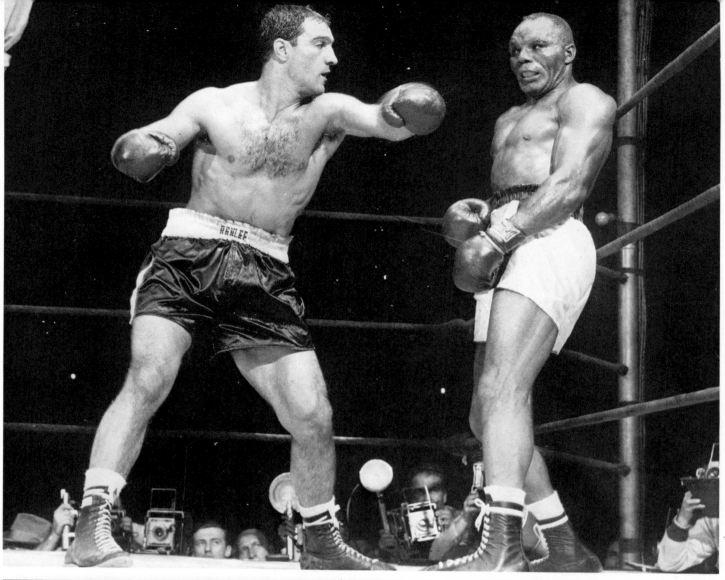

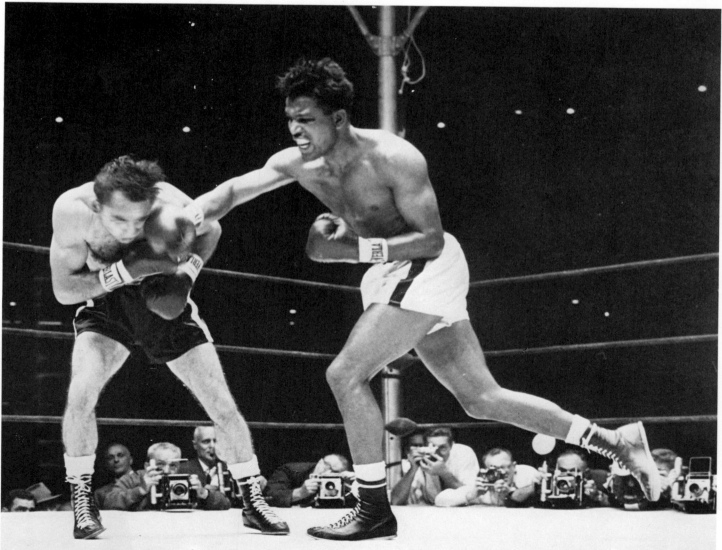

The Real Rocky

Champion Jersey Joe Walcott looked stunned by the vicious left of challenger Rocky Marciano in the 12th round of their bout in Philadelphia in 1952. He was.

But he held on, at least for another round.

Marciano knocked him out in the 13th round and took the title.

Sugar Attack

A snarling, determined, world middleweight champion Sugar Ray Robinson, mouthpiece flashing, connects with a long right to the face of crouching challenger Carmen Basilio in a title bout in 1957.

Determination wasn't enough, however. Basilio took a 15-round decision. But Sugar Ray got the title back from him the next year.

Greatest Game

There was 1:56 left in regulation, with the New York Giants ahead of the Baltimore Colts 17–14 for the 1958 NFL championship.

But it was enough time for quarterback Johnny Unitas, then 25 years old and just plucked from semi-pro ball by the Colts, to get his team from their own 14 yard line to the Giants' 13 and allow Steve Myhra to kick a tying field goal.

In the overtime period, the Giants got the ball but were forced to punt. The Colts took over on their own 20. The Giants never touched the ball on offense again.

With the play-calling of an experienced veteran, Unitas mixed up runs and sharp passing to get the Colts down to the 1 yard line. Eight minutes and 15 seconds into the first NFL sudden-death overtime game, Alan Ameche plunged over for the winning touchdown (on the ground, bottom left) before a crowd of more than 64,000 in Yankee Stadium.

The game, arguably the "greatest" in NFL history, vaulted Unitas to virtually instant fame.

Hungary For A Win

Laszlo Tabori of Hungary hit the tape just ahead of Britain's Chris Chataway to win the three-mile run in the British Games in August 1955. Tabori's time was 13 minutes, 44.6 seconds.

(The previous year, Chataway was second to Roger Bannister for Bannister's sub-four-minute mile, the first.)

Among the playing shirts retired by the Boston Celtics basketball franchise is No. 14. It belonged to Bob Cousy, here driving between Syracuse Nationals defenders John Kerr and Larry Costello in the 1959 NBA playoffs. (Cousy scored.)

Cousy was one of the most exciting players in the history of the game, a dazzling playmaker who averaged 18.5 points a game in 13 years with the Celtics. He was an All-Star in every one of those years and helped lead the Celtics to six NBA titles.

SIXTIES

The U.S. Open . . . the Masters . . . the British Open . . . golfing's tournaments of excellence.

The 1960s . . . the decade of Arnold Palmer . . . Jack Nicklaus . . . Gary Player . . . Lee Trevino . . . Billy Casper, Julius Boros, Tom Weiskopf, Frank Beard.

. . . of Bill Russell and the Boston Celtics . . . Y.A. Tittle, Jim Brown and Vince Lombardi . . . Ernie Banks . . . Sandy Koufax . . . Clemente and Mazeroski . . . and the New York Mets.

Arnold Palmer, who dominated the golf world in the late 1950s and early 1960s and was still on the circuit in the 1980s, is perhaps the most loved figure the sport ever produced.

With his boyish charm and his thrilling come-from-behind victories, he became the idol of a hero-worshipping flock known as "Arnie's Army."

Arnie and His Army

The rugged son of a greenskeeper from the steel town of Latrobe, Pennsylvania, Palmer built a reputation for being something of a miracle man on the links. "He literally wills the balls into the hole," his contemporaries said.

He won four Masters tournaments and one U.S. Open (in 1960), but never a PGA championship.

He built his golf success into a fortune worth millions.

His biggest rival over the years was Jack Nicklaus, 10 years his junior. In what many believe to be a turning point in the role of king of the game, Nicklaus beat Palmer in an 18-hole playoff for the U.S. Open championship in 1962.

The Golden Bear

Jack Nicklaus, it is generally agreed, is one of the most amazing superstars in any sport—a man who has dominated his field majestically for some 20 years.

There is hardly a record that the golfer hasn't held or doesn't hold, including 17 major triumphs (19 if his 2 U.S. Amateur crowns are counted); more than 69 tour victories; and over $4 million in official earnings. He won five PGAs, five Masters, four U.S. Opens, and three British Opens.

Here, the Golden Bear sinks a birdie putt on the 16th at Augusta National that led him to an unprecedented fifth Masters victory in 1975.

'Rocket Rod'

"Rocket" Rod Laver, red-headed left-hander from Australia, brought a new dimension to tennis with his slashing topspin shots and aggressive attack.

One of the all-time greats, he won two Wimbledon titles as an amateur in 1961 and 1962, then came back to win two more as a professional after Wimbledon became an open tournament, in 1968 and 1969.

In two of those years—1962 and 1969—he won the Grand Slam of tennis, the Australian, French and U.S. Opens and the Wimbledon.

Wooden Dynasty

The players read like a Who's Who of basketball: Walt Hazzard, Gail Goodrich, Lew Alcindor (Kareem Abdul-Jabbar), Sidney Wicks, Bill Walton.

The championships are unmatched in number and near-perfect sequence: 1964, 1965, 1967, 1968, 1969, 1970, 1971, 1972, 1973, 1975.

The team, of course, UCLA.

And the coach: John Wooden.

The soft-spoken, beloved coach retired with 10 NCAA championships and, in one period, an incredible record of 88 victories in a row.

He announced his retirement just before the championship game in 1975, and the team gave No. 10 and the victors net to the coach they called "the Man." It was a perfect going-away present for a great coach who had accomplished just about everything with a basketball team.

Among the 1,000 people who turned out to help Wooden celebrate his 75th birthday in 1980 were more than 100 former UCLA basketball players, including Bill Walton and Kareem Abdul-Jabbar.

Danger: Turn Ahead

The Indianapolis 500, America's traditional Memorial Day auto race, was in its 48th running in 1964. It had claimed 54 lives during those years.

"In the long run," driver Eddie Sachs had said, "death is the odds-on favorite."

On this Memorial Day, the leaders were headed into their third 2½-mile lap when Dave MacDonald lost control. His car hit the inside wall at 150 m.p.h. and bounced into the middle of the track. Blinded by the smoke and flames, six other drivers smacked into MacDonald's car.

One was Eddie Sachs.

Both he and MacDonald were killed.

'Mr. Defense'

Bill Russell of the Boston Celtics slammed one down the basket over arch-rival Wilt Chamberlain in a playoff game in 1969.

But it was defense that really earned Russell his all-time stardom.

Russell was acclaimed as the game's outstanding defensive player and shot blocker and was the hub of the Celtic dynasty in the late 1950s and 1960s.

His coach, Red Auerbach, once said of him, "He always made the big play. He developed the blocked shot into an art form. And he was team-oriented—all he wanted to do was win."

In balloting conducted by the Professional Basketball Writers Association of America in conjunction with the NBA's 35th anniversary in 1980, Russell was named the greatest player in the league's history.

Woody Hayes

Woody Hayes often said, "I just can't control my temper."

In 1978, that flaw spelled the end of a 36-year college football coaching career. He was fired after he slugged a Clemson player on the sidelines in Ohio State's 17–15 Gator Bowl loss.

He was 65 years old then, a victim of his own emotions, which had made him a center of controversy throughout his illustrious career. In 28 years at Ohio State, his teams had compiled a 205–61–10 record.

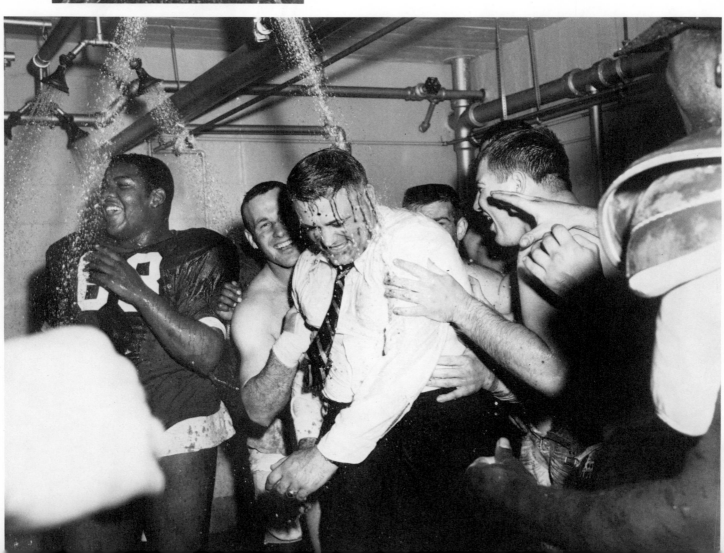

The Bear

When Paul Bryant was a teen-ager, a carnival came through his home town, As he told it, "They had this little old scraggly bear. A man was offering anybody a dollar a minute to wrestle it.

"I got the bear pinned, holdin' on tight. The man kept whispering, 'Let him up. Let him up.' Hell, for a dollar a minute I wanted to hold him til he died."

Thus, did Paul Bryant earn the nickname "Bear," which stayed with him through all his years as the winningest college football coach of all time.

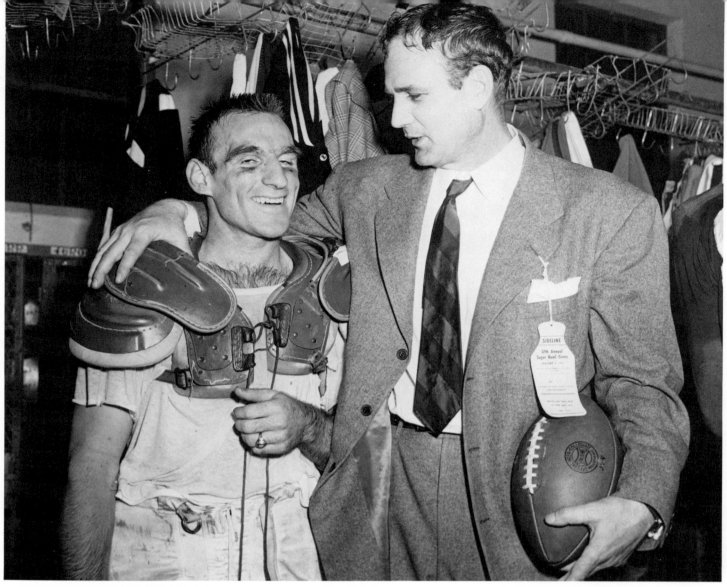

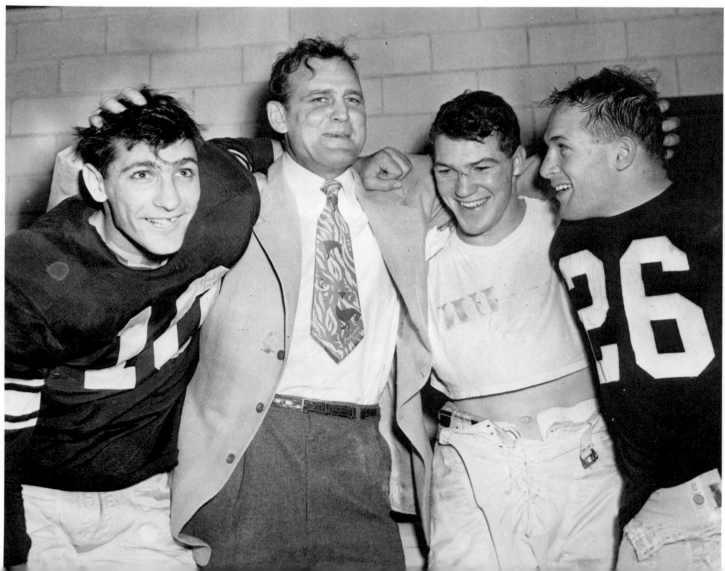

When he died in 1983 at the age 69, four weeks after his last victory and six weeks after announcing his retirement, his coaching record was 232–85–17, a mark that will be remembered—if not stand—as long as football is played.

He began coaching at the University of Maryland in 1945, went on to Kentucky, then Texas A&M before going to Alabama in 1958. It was a quarter of a century before Alabama would need another coach. During those years, he coached the likes of future pro quarterbacks Joe Namath, Ken Stabler, and Richard Todd and led Alabama to five national championships.

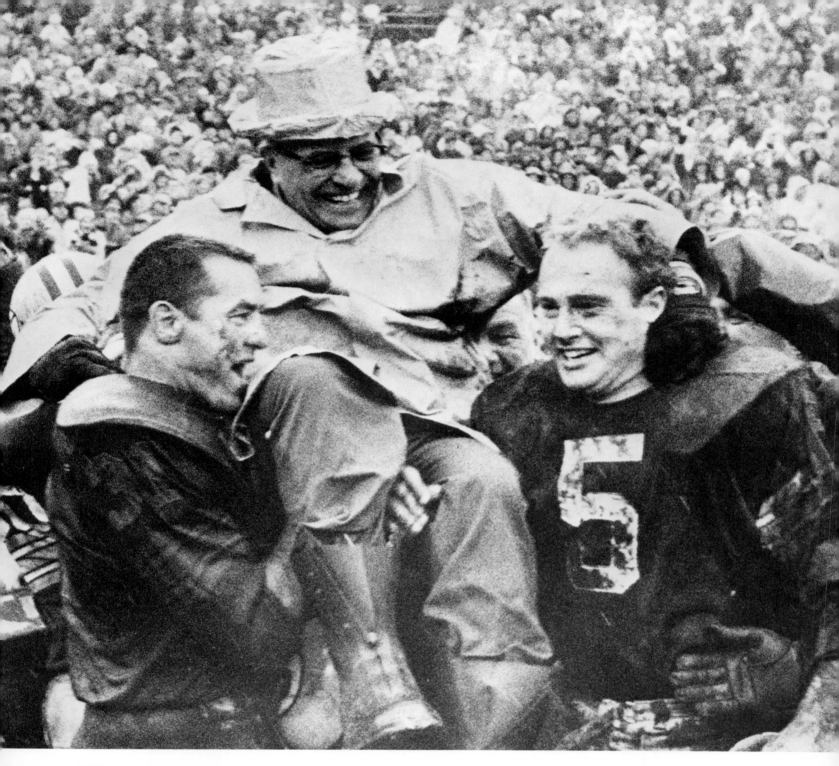

'Winning Isn't Everything . . . '

" . . . It's the only thing."

That motto on the importance of victory has become synonymous with the man who believed it and lived by it, football coach Vince Lombardi.

The tough taskmaster got the most out of his teams; his nine-year coaching record with the Green Bay Packers was 89–29–4. He built the Packers into a world champion football dynasty in the 1960s, with NFL titles in 1961, 1962, 1965, 1966, and 1967. His Packers also won the first two Super Bowls against American Football League teams, with the likes of quarterback Bart Starr and running backs Jim Taylor (No. 31) and Paul Hornung (5), carrying Lombardi on their shoulders in this picture taken after they won the 1966 NFL title.

Marshalling the Wrong Forces

Jim Marshall, defensive end for the Minnesota Vikings, scooped up a fumble by the San Francisco 49ers in a September 1964 game.

He took it 60 yards to the end zone.

The wrong end zone.

There he was congratulated by Bruce Bosley of the 49ers for scoring two points, a safety, for them.

It took a long while for Marshall to live down that embarrassing moment, but he became one of the greatest defensemen in the NFL as part of the Vikings' "Purple People Eaters" defense of the late 1960s.

'Big, Bad' Jimmy Brown

Jimmy Brown, the great Cleveland Browns running back, did it his way, but many believe there will never be any to match him.

Elected to the Hall of Fame in 1971, Brown gained a career 12,312 yards in nine seasons.

A fellow Hall of Famer, Andy Robustelli, paid him this tribute: "He had quickness, speed, strength, flexibility. He was relaxed, very poised, and he was a determined guy. You just never get the speed, shiftiness, and elusiveness he had at 220 pounds, coupled with such a great temperament."

Robustelli played defense for the New York Giants when Brown's achievements were at the top.

"I don't want to minimize any of the kids today," Robustelli said years later, "but in 1960, at the height of Jimmy's career, the league was at a peak with a minimum of 12 teams and a maximum of quality players selected from all the colleges in the country."

Brown, who retired to pursue a movie career led the league in rushing for eight seasons (1957–61, 1963–65).

Work Daze

Maybe this is why professional quarterbacks are highly paid.

Y. A. (Yelverton Abraham) Tittle was running the New York Giants offense in the early 1960s—and running it to three division championships—when he ran into the Pittsburgh Steelers early in the 1964 season.

The 38-year-old passer was knocked down by 270-pound John Baker. The ball popped loose. Steeler tackle Chuck Hinton picked it up and ran six yards for a touchdown.

Tittle, the classic picture of dazed futility, was bleeding from two cuts on his head and felt the pain in his ribs. It was weeks before he was back in the lineup.

Star Running Back

Gale Sayers played only seven years in the National Football League, but he made the impression of a lifetime spent there.

The Chicago Bears running back scored an NFL record 22 touchdowns as a rookie in 1965—six of them coming in one game. The next year he rushed for a career-high 1,231 yards.

The first of his serious knee injuries sidelined him for much of the 1968 season, but he had another 1,000-yard campaign in 1969 before the injuries began to mount up and his brilliant career was cut short.

Here, the Hall of Famer runs 20 yards for a TD against the Detroit Lions in 1965.

Roger, A Record

It was October 1, 1961, the 162nd and last regular-season game of the year for the New York Yankees. If Roger Maris were ever to do it, it had to be now.

On this second time at bat, in the fourth inning, facing Boston Red Sox pitcher Tracy Stallard, the 27-year-old Yankee outfielder became the first player in major league history to hit more than 60 home runs in a season. It surpassed Babe Ruth's mark of 60, made in 1927, in a 154-game season.

Artistically enough, the home run was a winning one, as the Yankees triumphed, 1–0.

89

Perfect Pitcher

No-hitters are rarities, but Sandy Koufax tried to make an annual habit of it.

The Brooklyn-born Dodger left-hander threw one in 1962, 1963, and 1964. For an encore, he pitched a perfect no-hitter in 1965—a year in which he struck out 382 batters.

Koufax started out pitching for the University of Cincinnati. He never played in the minor leagues, but joined the then-Brooklyn Dodgers in 1955 and retired in 1966 as one of the greatest pitchers in baseball history.

His perfect game, which the Los Angeles Dodgers won, 1–0, was September 9, 1965, against the Chicago Cubs.

He struck out 15 batters in a 1963 World Series game and was the National League's Most Valuable Player that year. He was the Cy Young award winner as the best pitcher in baseball in 1963, 1965, and 1966.

Roberto Clemente

When Roberto Clemente played in the 1971 World Series, Roger Angell wrote of him, "He played a kind of baseball that none of us had ever seen before—throwing and running and hitting at something close to the level of perfection, playing to win but also playing as if it were a form of punishment for everyone else on the field."

Another once described him as "the most complete baseball player" ever.

It was a great loss when Roberto Clemente died at the age of 38, in a plane crash off the coast of his native Puerto Rico. He was on his way to help earthquake victims in Nicaragua.

Clemente won four National League batting titles as an outfielder for the Pittsburgh Pirates. He got 3,000 hits in his career, with a .317 lifetime average. He won the league's Most Valuable Player award in 1966 and played on 12 All-Star teams in an 18-year career. He was admired for his fine fielding and throwing as well as his hitting.

In this sequence, he makes a sensational backhanded catch off a poke by Bobby Thomson of the Chicago Cubs in a 1958 game.

Triple Threat

A triple portrait of batting stars is offered in this picture of three baseball greats, from left to right: Mickey Mantle, Stan Musial, Roger Maris. They met before a New York Yankees-St. Louis Cardinals exhibition game in March 1962.

Home Is the Hero

Pittsburgh Pirates fans rushed onto the field right behind their favorite players to celebrate Bill Mazeroski's World Series-winning home run in 1960.

The Pirate second baseman hit it in the bottom of the ninth to defeat the New York Yankees, 10–9, in the seventh and deciding game.

Amazin'

In 1962, when they were created, the New York Mets were undoubtedly the saddest team in baseball.

Their original manager, Casey Stengel, wondered aloud, "Can't anybody here play this game?"

In 1969, the Mets won the World Series.

Amazing.

Led by the pitching of Tom Seaver and Jerry Koosman, the hitting of the likes of Tommie Agee—and the unlikely Al Weis—and some timely super catches by Ron Swoboda, the Mets beat the Baltimore Orioles in five games.

Swing Time

San Francisco Giant pitcher Juan Marichal, wearing No. 27, was upset when Los Angeles Dodger catcher John Roseboro apparently threw too close to his head in returning a pitched ball to Sandy Koufax in a Candlestick Park game in August 1965.

Marichal swung at Roseboro. Koufax (No. 32) almost got it instead, as he came in to help Roseboro.

Banks On It

Ernie Banks was "Mr. Cub" for most of the 19 years he played for the Chicago Cubs. He wouldn't have had it any other way.

To Banks, Wrigley Field was beautiful; just playing baseball in the daytime was beautiful. "Let's play two," he would say on the brighter sunshine days.

"To Ernie Banks," AP's Will Grimsely once wrote, "playing baseball was like waking up every day to a pile of toys under a Christmas tree. It was sunshine, hot dogs, old family friends, dedication, loyalty, a 20th century Camelot."

The Hall of Famer returned it all with his talents. The Cub shortstop hit 512 home runs in his career and was the only shortstop ever to lead his league in homers and fielding (in 1960).

Here, in a 1967 game against the St. Louis Cardinals, he acknowledges cheers for his 2,500th base hit, off Bob Gibson.

And Howe . . .

Gordie Howe did everything on ice that a hockey player must do—and he did most of those things with a special flair that set him apart from other players.

In 1971, this hockey legend retired from the game after 25 with the Detroit Red Wings. But two years later Gordie Howe was back with the Houston Aeros of the World Hockey Association. The lure was the chance to play with his sons, Mark and Marty. Then, he moved on to play with the New England Whalers.

When the NHL Hall of Famer finally called it quits as an active player, he had 1,071 goals in both NHL and WHA regular-season and playoff games, 1,518 assists, and 2,589 points.

Numbers that may never be matched.

In this photo, Howe falls on an interception in a 1968 game against the New York Rangers and kept the puck rolling as the Red Wings won, 4–2. Howe didn't score in the game, but he had collected the 700th goal of his career the previous night in Pittsburgh.

Barefoot Boy With Victory

Abebe Bikila of Ethiopia ran in his bare feet to win the Olympic marathon in Rome in 1960. And in then-record time: 2 hours, 15 minutes, 16.2 seconds.

Abdesian Rhadi of Morocco was second.

Bikila won the marathon again in Tokyo in 1964, in 2:12:11.2. But with shoes.

Meters Man

The place didn't matter; neither did the competition.

Peter Snell of New Zealand seemed to "own" the 800-meter race.

Wearing No. 83, Snell set a then-Olympic record time for the event in Rome in 1960, with a 1:46.3.

Four years later, he won the gold again, in the same event in the Tokyo Olympics, racing in 1:45.1.

Road to Rome

World champion miler Herb Elliott of Australia showed one reason why he was among the best.

In training for the Olympics in Rome in 1960, he started with an eight-mile barefoot run along the beach and through the brush. He followed that with a weight-lifting session. Then he did five miles of roadwork.

At the time, he held the record for the mile, 3:54.5, which he set in Dublin, Ireland, two years earlier in a race in which all five runners finished in under four minutes.

Behind Elliott were Merv Lincoln of Australia, Murray Halberg (dark shirt) of New Zealand, Albert Thomas of Australia, and Ron Delany of Ireland and Villanova, Pennsylvania.

How did Elliott do in the Rome Olympics? He won the 1,500-meter race in 3:35.6.

L - O - N - G Jump

Bob Beamon of El Paso, Texas, dug his feet into a world record for the long jump in the Mexico City Olympics of 1968.
He leaped 29 feet 2½ inches on his first attempt.

Ceremonial Symbol

Let the Games begin.

    The symbol of the ancient Olympic Games is carried by Yoshinori Sakai, as he carries the torch to the caldron at the National Stadium during the opening ceremony of the Tokyo Games in October 1964.

Ski-lly

The name Jean-Claude Killy was synonymous with Alpine skiing since his 1968 Olympic sweep of three gold medals at Grenoble in his native France.

Here, he shows the winning style at giant slalom in Germany in 1966.

A Winning Year

Denny McLain, Detroit Tigers right-hander, was the unanimous choice for the Cy Young award in the American League in 1968.

Little wonder. He won 31 games that year.

Here, he beat the Oakland A's, 4–1, for his 18th win of the season.

McLain posted a 31–6 record—the first man to win 30 games in a season since Dizzy Dean—with a 1.96 earned run average. He led the Tigers to the American League pennant and won the AL's Most Valuable Player award along with the Cy Young.

The right-hander was 24–9 in 1969 and was named co-winner of the Cy Young award with Baltimore's Mike Cuellar. McLain also was a 20-game winner in 1966.

His major league career plunged after the 1969 season, however, and he left baseball in 1972.

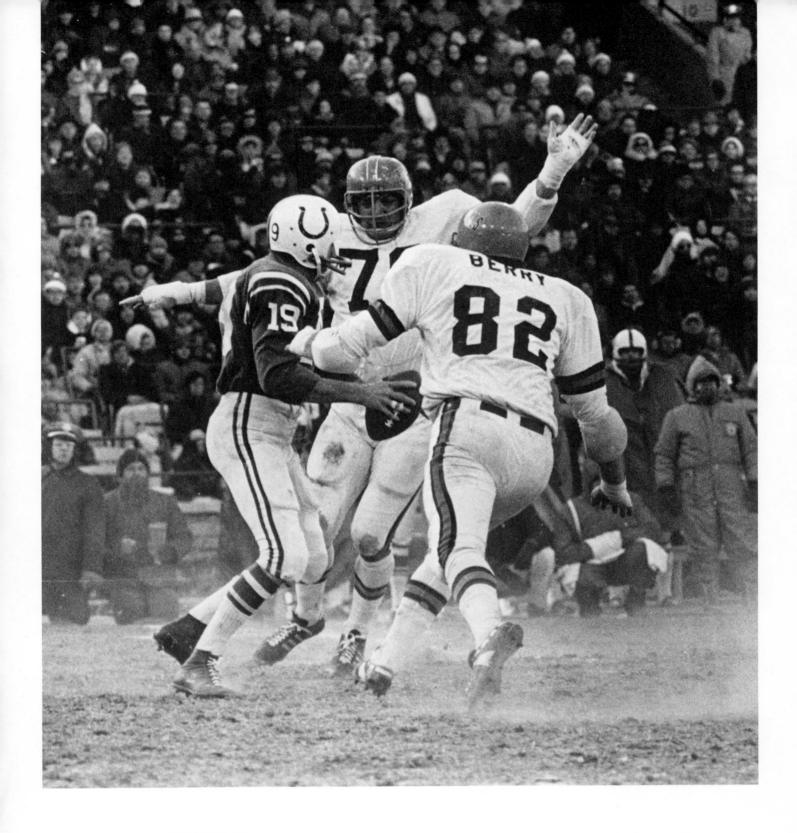

Johnny U

Johnny Unitas and the Baltimore Colts were synonymous in the 1960s.

The Hall of Fame quarterback played 17 years with the Colts and led them to two Super Bowl appearances.

In his 18-year NFL career, Unitas recorded a string of 47 consecutive games in which he threw for at least one touchdown. He also threw for more than 300 yards in a game 26 times in his career.

WEATHER...
OR NOT

It was the end of a gloomy day for the Baltimore Colts as Paul Hornung of the Green Bay Packers raced 65 yards with a pass from Bart Starr for his fifth touchdown of the day. Green Bay won the December 1965 game, 42–27, in the fog at Baltimore's Memorial Stadium.

Snowtime in the Rockies. A heavy snowstorm seemed to help the Denver Broncos this day as they huddled for the last two minutes in a 1979 game against the New England Patriots. The scoreboard shows the final score, 45–10.

How cold was it? It was so cold that breaths seemed to hang in the air, frozen, as was most everything else.

The Cincinnati Bengals and San Diego Chargers faced off in sub-zero temperatures for the AFC championship game in Cincinnati in 1982. The Bengals won, 27–7.

A soggy day in Washington town. Plastered with mud, Philadelphia Eagles halfback Tom Brookshier comes up for air after a play against the Washington Redskins in December 1957.

  The Redskins won, 42–7.

Saint Joseph High School of Atlanta didn't let a downpour rain out their game in November 1966. John Blackwell is mute evidence that the field was a sea of mud.

University of Pennsylvania players are smeared with mud after a game with Cornell University in Philadelphia in November 1950.

  They lost, too, 13–6.

SEVENTIES

The Big Men in basketball . . . Wilt Chamberlain and Kareem Abdul-Jabbar at the top of the the game . . .
  UCLA and John Wooden—and ten NCAA championships.
  And Seattle Slew, Affirmed and Alydar, Secretariat, Spectacular Bid.
  Joe Namath and O.J. Simpson.
  Muhammad Ali.
  Seaver . . . Bench . . . Yaz . . . Aaron . . . Reggie . . . Brooks . . .
  And Pele.

Gold Rush

The Munich Olympics, 1972.
    Swimmer Mark Spitz, of Carmichael, California, became the first ever to win five gold medals in a single Olympics. he took the 100-meter butterfly, the 100-meter freestyle, was part of the 400-meter freestyle relay, and won the 200-meter freestyle and the 200-meter butterfly.

Broadway Joe

The New York Jets were the upstarts in an upstart new league, the American Football League.

But when Joe Willie Namath was playing quarterback, anything could happen.

The Alabama, Bear Bryant-trained passer was considered among the finest when he signed up.

In 1969, he predicted the Jets would win the Super Bowl and be the first in the AFL to do it. His talent was as good as his boast. The Jets beat the heavily favored Baltimore Colts, 16–7, in Super Bowl III.

"Broadway Joe" was as flamboyant off the field as on, shocking the football establishment by wearing a goatee, then shaving it off for $10,000; ushering a constant bevy of beautiful women; and enjoying to the hilt being Joe Namath.

When he put his white shoes, gimpy knees, and familiar No. 12 into retirement in 1978, the playboy quarterback from Beaver Falls, Pennsylvania, had been named AFL Rookie of the Year (1965); passed for 4,007 yards in the 1967 season; and combined with quarterback Johnny Unitas of the Colts for 872 passing yards in one game in 1972 (Namath threw for six touchdowns in that game).

Spectacular

Jockey Ronnie Franklin raised his whip at the finish line as Spectacular Bid did what he did best—win.

The horse simply ran away from four 3-year-old rivals at Pimlico to win the 1979 Preakness with the second fastest clocking in the history of the race, completing the mile and three-sixteenths in 1:54 1/5. That was just a fifth of a second off the track and stakes record set by Canonero II in 1971.

Spectacular Bid, who also won the Kentucky Derby in 1979 and was a winner in 21 of 25 races in his career, was syndicated in 1980 for $22 million.

O.J.

This one put him over the top.

The familiar No. 32 on the jersey of O. J. Simpson of the Buffalo Bills starts a carry of seven yards in a game against the New York Jets in December 1973.

The yardage gave "Juice" 200 yards in the game and a season total of 2,003. Quarterback Joe Ferguson is behind him, and running back Jim Braxton blocked out Jets defensive tackle Steve Thompson (87) for the run that made Simpson the first in NFL history to gain more than 2,000 yards in a season.

Simpson retired from football in 1979 to close out his career with 11,236 yards. He played nine years with the Buffalo Bills before being traded to the San Francisco 49ers. O. J. (Orenthel James) had made his reputation in California, as a star running back with USC.

King Pelé

Probably no one—no one—has ever dominated a sport as well for as long as Edson Arantes de Nascimento, the man known the world over as Pelé.

The king of soccer played for 22 years, in 1,363 games, and scored a record 1,281 goals—more than twice as many as any other player—before retiring in 1977.

Pelé, the "Black Pearl," led his native Brazil to an unprecedented three World Cups. After retiring from the Santos national team in 1974, Pelé signed with the New York Cosmos, leading them to a North American Soccer League title in 1977 and helping to popularize the sport throughout the United States.

The man with the magic feet was revered as an athlete the world over.

"People have said that Pelé has no religion, nationality, or color," he once said of himself. "I have been accepted everywhere. I would like to be remembered as a person who showed the world that the simplicity of a man is still the most important quality. Through simplicity and sincerity can you put all humankind together."

Pelé, the king.

Gymnastic Grace

Grace on the balance beam was personified by gymnast Cathy Rigby in the 1972 Olympics in Munich, Germany. The California star was then 19 years old.

Miss Rigby was the United States' top female gymnast at the 1968 Olympics at Mexico City as well as at Munich. Then, she turned professional, putting her gymnastic talent and dance training to use first in a musical production of *Peter Pan*.

A Standout Performance

Nadia Comaneci of Romania, the outstanding gymnast of the 1976 Olympics in Montreal, demonstrated her form on the balance beam.

Wilt the Stilt

Wilt Chamberlain was an awesome figure on the basketball court: 7 feet 1 inch and 275 pounds when he was trimmed down.

Without argument, he was one of the greatest ever to play the game.

Chamberlain was a high school sensation at Overbrook in Philadelphia, became an All-American at Kansas University, then quit college in 1958 to tour with the Harlem Globetrotters.

In 1959, he signed with the NBA's Philadelphia Warriors, launching a record-smashing career that spanned 15 years.

Chamberlain was the first basketball player of his height and strength who also had the speed and dexterity of smaller men. He earned the nickname "the Big Dipper" for his dunk shots.

He scored a total of 31,419 points in his career (a record broken by Kareem Abdul-Jabbar in 1984) and pulled down 23,924 rebounds, a record to this day.

At the Top of His Game

Kareem Abdul-Jabbar grew up in New York City as Lew Alcindor and had an extraordinary high school career at Power Memorial.

In college, he led UCLA to three consecutive NCAA titles (1967–69) and was the tournament's Most Valuable Player all three years.

His success grew in the National Basketball Association. He began with the Milwaukee Bucks in 1969 and was voted the league's Rookie of the Year. The 7-foot-2 center played six seasons with the Bucks before being traded to the Los Angeles Lakers. For religious reasons, he changed his name from Lew Alcindor in 1971.

He's won six league MVP awards and has been selected to play in the All-Star game 14 times through 1984, the year he broke Wilt Chamberlain's all-time career scoring record.

In 1985, at the age of 38, he led the Lakers to the NBA Championship in six games over the Boston Celtics, and set the all-time playoff scoring record, previously held by former Laker teammate Jerry West.

The Big Men

Some of the biggest and best in basketball go at it against each other in these photos.

In the photo taken from above, 'Sixer Moses Malone and Laker Kareem Abdul-Jabbar don't look the 7-foot-plus that they are. They squared off for the NBA championship in 1983.

Clown Prince of Golf

Bouncy, ebullient Lee Trevino was considered the clown prince of big-time golf.

During a practice round before the start of the U.S. Open golf championship in 1971, he put on a marshal's hat and joked it up with a rubber snake and a hatchet in the Merion Golf Club rough.

But, then he got serious and shot a 2-under-par 68 to beat Jack Nicklaus in their 18-hole playoff for the championship.

The popular Mexican-American golfer is generally loose and uninhibited and quick with the quip.

"He is to golf," AP's Will Grimsley once wrote, "what Yogi Berra and Dizzy Dean have been to baseball. . . . He has enriched the game with both his skill and his 'Trevinoisms.' "

Indy Tragedy

The car driven by Swede Savage, a Californian, rammed the wall and exploded during the Indianapolis 500 race in 1973. Savage was killed.

Fairest of Them All

"I didn't know if it was going to be fair or foul—but I knew if it was fair, it was out of here."

Boston Red Sox catcher Carlton Fisk had come to the plate to lead off the 12th inning of the tied sixth game of the 1975 World Series in Boston. Facing Cincinnati Reds relief pitcher Pat Darcy, Fisk looked up to see which way the wind was blowing, perhaps hoping for a little help if he got a ball up in the air.

When he did hit it, he didn't need any help from the wind as far as distance was concerned. The only question was fair or foul.

Fisk stood near the plate for a moment, hoping, trying to wave it fair. Finally, it hit the screen—on the fair side of the pole atop the left field wall—and the Red Sox had won, 7–6, and tied the Series at three games apiece.

Cincinnati went on to win the Series in the seventh game, but few will ever forget the emotional and dramatic sixth game and Fisk's suspenseful deciding blow.

The Baseball Bird

Mark Fidrych was a happy-go-lucky kid in a Harpo Marx hairdo who talked to baseballs, manicured the mound on his hands and knees, and blew bubbles in the dugout.

He could pitch, too.

In 1976, "the Bird" had a 19–9 record with the Detroit Tigers, led the American League with a 2.34 earned run average and 24 complete games, and was named AL Rookie of the Year.

But his bubble soon burst, with a knee injury and recurring arm troubles, and by 1982 he was out of baseball.

"I had ten great years of baseball," Fidrych said, "no matter if it was the minor leagues or the major leagues. I got ten years out of my life where I got to do what I wanted to do, play baseball."

Net, As In Nettles

To the opposition, it seemed as though Graig Nettles played with a net, not an ordinary glove.

The third baseman, who played most of his career with the New York Yankees, earned fame as a slick fielder—and hit more home runs than any third baseman in American League history. He gained nationwide recognition in the 1978 World Series against the Los Angeles Dodgers when he turned the Series around in the third game with his spectacular fielding. He led the American League with 32 home runs in 1976 and hit a career high 37 home runs the next year. He was named Yankee captain in 1982, and was traded to the San Diego Padres in 1984.

The Man With The Golden Glove

When Brooks Robinson retired from baseball in 1977, he was considered the greatest third baseman of his time.

Here, he shows why. The Baltimore Oriole made a diving catch of a Johnny Bench line drive in the ninth inning of the final game of the 1970 World Series against the Cincinnati Reds. The Orioles won the game and the Series, one of four World Series that the popular No. 5 played in.

Robinson was simply brilliant in the field, earning a string of 16 consecutive Gold Glove awards from 1960 through 1975. In 23 illustrious seasons beginning with the Orioles in 1955, Robinson also had 2,848 hits and 268 home runs. He was named the American League's Most Valuable Player in 1964 and was the MVP of the 1970 World Series.

Johnny Bench, Catcher

Few who dream of becoming major league baseball players see themselves encumbered by a mask, shin guards, and chest protector. Few want to be catchers.

But when Johnny Bench was honored at his retirement at Cincinnati's Riverfront Stadium in 1983, he chose to go behind the plate and, with tired legs and sore glove hand, crouch one more time.

"Catching made me, and I made catching," said the 14-time All-Star. "I may not have been Johnny Bench if it wasn't for catching."

Some of his adventures in catching are shown here: Bench scaling the wall and net behind the plate to haul in a pop foul in St. Louis in 1972; Bench holding on to a throw despite a collision with Chicago Cubs runner Dave Kingman, who tried unsuccessfully to score from third on an infield grounder.

Bench did quite well with the bat as well as behind the bat.

In addition to winning 10 consecutive Gold Gloves for fielding, he led the National League in 1970 with 45 home runs and 148 runs batted in. In his 16-year career, he had 325 homers, a record for a catcher; 389 career homers; was National League Most Valuable Player in 1970 and 1972, and World Series MVP in 1976.

Yaz

"Somewhere men are laughing, and somewhere children shout. But there is no joy in Fenway—mighty Yaz is bowing out."

Thus did Boston Red Sox fan Edward M. Kennedy, the Democratic senator from Massachusetts, borrow from Ernest Lawrence Thayer's poem to join the tributes to Carl Yastrzemski, "Captain Carl," the 23 year Red Sox slugger who retired after the 1983 season at the age of 44.

Yaz, who started out as a shortstop, was moved to left field and replaced Ted Williams there in 1961. He played in more than 3,300 games, leading his team to pennants in 1967 and 1975 and earning seven Gold Gloves for his fielding.

That famous glove is misplaced in this photo, as Yaz, playing first base in a 1976 game against the New York Yankees, leaps for a high pickoff throw and loses the mitt in the attempt.

Tom Terrific

Tom Seaver may be wearing a Cincinnati Reds uniform in these photos, but more than any other single person, "Tom Terrific" typified the Amazin' Mets of 1969.

When he came to the Mets in 1967, the popular pitcher became the first ever to win Rookie of the Year honors for a last-place club. Two years later, he helped propel them to the first of two National League pennants and later the "miracle" World Series championship. In 1969, the strikeout sensation posted a 25–7 record and a 2.21 ERA.

He won three Cy Young pitching awards and five times won 20 or more games for the Mets, but was traded to the Cincinnati Reds in 1977.

Ironically, it was there that he pitched the only no-hitter of his career, in a 1978 game against the St. Louis Cardinals.

The Mets re-acquired him in 1983 but he was drafted by the Chicago White Sox the next year in the free-agent compensation pool.

Big Daddy

When the Pittsburgh Pirates of the late 1970s claimed, "We are family," there was little question of who Daddy was: Willie Stargell.

On October 3, 1982, the 41-year-old "Pops" beat out an infield single in his final time at bat in a 20-year career with the Pirates. He left the game to a standing ovation, with the stadium organist playing "Pomp and Circumstance," and the fans calling him out of the dugout for a final curtain call. The popular player was mobbed by his teammates as he left the field.

Stargell had joined the Pirates in 1962 after signing a free-agent contract for a $1,500 bonus in 1958. He played on two Pirates world championship teams, in 1971 and 1979, and was the Most Valuable Player in both the National League Championship series and World Series in 1979.

He finished his career with 475 home runs, tied with Stan Musial on the all-time career home-run list.

Here, the Bucs captain hits a homer in the sixth inning of the final game of the 1979 World Series in Baltimore, and leaps for joy after recording the last out at first base in the second game. The Bucs won both games and the Series.

You Make the Call

In the first game of the 1970 World Series, Cincinnati Red Bernie Carbo slid toward home. Baltimore Oriole catcher Elrod Hendricks held the ball and tagged him with the glove.
  Umpire Ken Burkhart was caught in the middle.
  His call? *Out!*

Record Round-Tripper

A special moment in sports history.
  Henry Aaron of the Atlanta Braves, on his second time at bat in a game against the Los Angeles Dodgers on April 8, 1974, hits a 1–0 fastball off Al Downing out of Atlanta Stadium for a home rum.
  But not just a home run. It was Aaron's 715th, the one that put him ahead of Babe Ruth at the top of the career home-run list. There were 40 more from his bat before he retired.

Gone . . . Gone . . . and Gone Again

In the sixth game of the 1977 World Series against the Los Angeles Dodgers, New York Yankee Reggie Jackson had hit a home run off Burt Hooten in the fourth inning. Then he hit another in the fifth inning off reliever Elias Sosa.

Could he do it again? No one else ever had hit three consecutive homers in one Series game.

He sure could. And did. In the eighth inning, off Charlie Hough, Jackson gave the Yankees an 8–4 win, their 21st World Series championship—and took his own place in the record book.

The Winning Smile

Nancy Lopez displayed the winner's form as she sank her putt on the ninth hole of the third round of the Ladies Professional Golf Association Championship in Mason, Ohio, in 1978. It dropped for a birdie.

She was Player of the Year in women's golf that year, winning nine of the 25 tournaments in which she competed—five of them in a sensational summer streak.

Her 71.76 scoring average was the best in the history of the LPGA, exceeding the top efforts of such greats as Babe Zaharias, Mickey Wright, and Kathy Whitworth.

Record Run

Archie Griffin of Ohio State finished off a 22-yard run in a 1974 game against Illinois, entering the record books by gaining 100 yards or more for 18 straight games. He was just a junior then.

The 5-foot 9-inch tailback, major college football's first 5,000-yard runner, was also the first two-time winner of the Heisman Trophy, in 1974 and 1975.

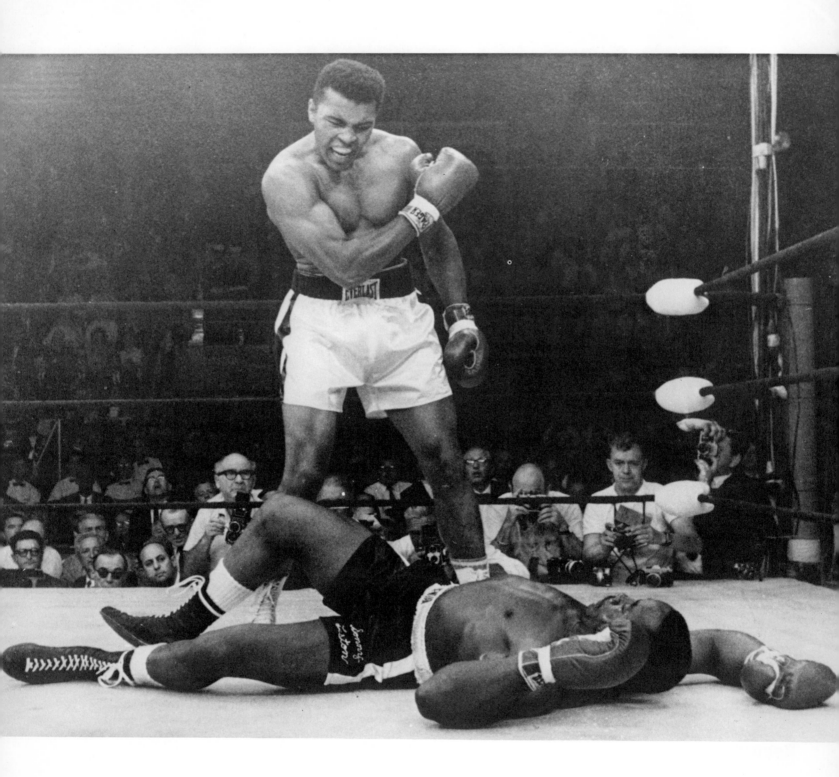

The Name Is Ali . . . and I Sting Like A Bee

The man born as Cassius Clay boasted in verse.

"I float like a butterfly and sting like a bee."

Brash loudmouth, many said.

But "the lip" made good his boasts.

He won the heavyweight boxing title an unprecedented three times. One of his most memorable fights was in defense of the championship in a rematch against Sonny Liston in Lewiston, Maine, in 1965.

The fight lasted only one minute. Clay flattened Liston with a short hard right to the jaw—his "phantom punch," he said. The 218-pound Liston went down like a rock, fell on his back, rolled over, got to one knee, but fell back again, to stay.

The gloating Clay stood over the vanquished Liston, screaming, "Get up, you bum!"

Clay took on the Muslim religion and changed his name to Muhammad Ali. He remained a controversial figure throughout his career.

Stripped of his title for his refusal to accept the military draft, he was idle in 1968 and 1969, but he was later exonerated and began a comeback. He knocked out Jerry Quarry in 1970, then challenged Joe Frazier.

In that Madison Square Garden bout on March 8, 1971, Frazier knocked down Ali in the 15th round, as referee Arthur Mercante gestured to the victor. It was Ali's first title loss.

But Ali came back to flatten George Foreman in a title fight in Zaire in 1974, then defended the crown 11 times—including the "Thrilla in Manila," in which he stopped Frazier in 14 rounds in October 1975.

He lost the title once again—at the age of 38—to Leon Spinks in 1978, but came back later that year to regain it.

Most finally agreed with his boast: "I am the greatest!"

Secretariat

Secretariat captured the hearts of millions in 1973, winning the first Triple Crown in 25 years, since Citation.

He was Horse of the Year in 1972 and again in 1973, winning nine of 12 starts overall, a second twice, and a third once.

The champion 3 year old colt won the 1973 Belmont Stakes by 31 lengths, the biggest lead in the history of the event.

Here, jockey Ron Turcotte stands in the saddle as Secretariat crosses the finish line alone to win the Derby.

Double Dynamite

Affirmed and Alydar.

It was hard to tell the difference between the two great horses that matched up against each other in the 1978 Belmont Stakes—one of the best horse races in history.

The difference between the two at the end was "about three inches," according to Alydar's trainer, John Veitch.

In winning—officially by a head—Affirmed won the 11th Triple Crown in horse-racing history, a title that also includes the Kentucky Derby and the Preakness.

Alydar finished second in all three races that year.

Eighteen-year-old jockey Steve Cauthen, on Affirmed, became the youngest ever to win the Triple Crown—and in his first attempt.

Affirmed's time was 2:26 4–5, just 2-4/5 seconds off the world record set by Secretariat in winning the Belmont and Triple Crown in 1973. The win was the narrowest of any by a Triple Crown winner victor in the Belmont.

A Slew of Wins

From the top:

Seattle Slew wins the Kentucky Derby, May 7

Seattle Slew wins the Preakness Stakes, May 21

Seattle Slew wins the Belmont Stakes, June 12.

The latter put Seattle Slew on the list of immortals in thoroughbred horse racing. It was his ninth consecutive victory in 1977 and made him the only undefeated Triple Crown winner.

Jockey Jean Cruguet was up in all three races.

Drag Race Death

Cameraman Joe Rooks, of Bowling Green, Ohio, was filming the National Hot Rod Association Nationals in Indianapolis on September 1, 1979, when a dragster driven by Frank Rupert turned over several times and smashed into the rail.

Parts of the car flew into the field. The engine supercharger bounced up and hit Rooks in the back. He died on the way to the hospital. Rupert suffered a broken leg and internal injuries.

Immaculate Reception

Franco Harris played 12 NFL seasons with the Pittsburgh Steelers, amassing close to 12,000 yards as a running back for the team, but perhaps none of his runs was as memorable as this one against the Oakland Raiders in the 1972 American Conference playoffs.

Trailing the play on a desperation pass to teammate John Fuqua, Harris caught a caroming football off the shoulder pad of Raider defender Jack Tatum and romped 42 yards to beat the Raiders, 13–7. There were five seconds left in the game.

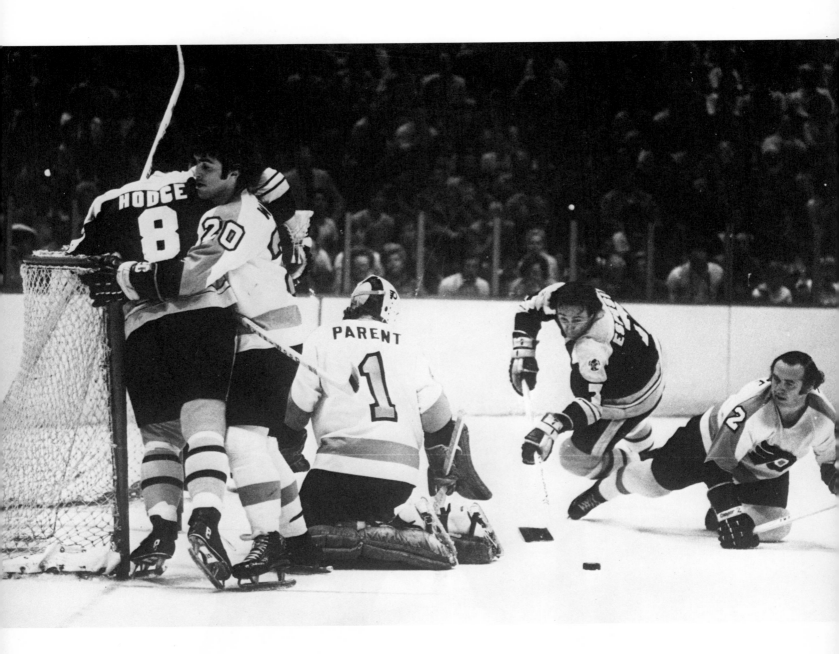

The Iceman

For 17 years, Phil Esposito was one of hockey's dominant players.

He entered the NHL in 1963, but made his reputation as a scorer after being traded from Chicago to the Boston Bruins in 1967. In 1968–69, he became the first player to score 100 points, winding up with 49 goals and 77 assists. That was the first of Esposito's six straight seasons as a First-Team All-Star, and he also was the NHL's Most Valuable Player. He won the MVP award again in 1973–74.

He was traded to the New York Rangers before he retired in 1981.

He's shown in action as the Bruins center in a game against the Philadelphia Flyers in 1974.

Billie Jean

In the mid and late 1960s, women's tennis seemed a two-woman battle between a tall, reserved Australian named Margaret Smith Court and a bouncy, outgoing Californian: Billie Jean Moffitt King.

Mrs. Court won 11 Australian championships, six American, five French and three Wimbledons.

But the dynamic Billie Jean King triumphed six times at Wimbledon, where she always seemed to play her best tennis. She took three titles in a row (1966-68) and three out of four in the early 1970s.

She also had four U.S. Open championships.

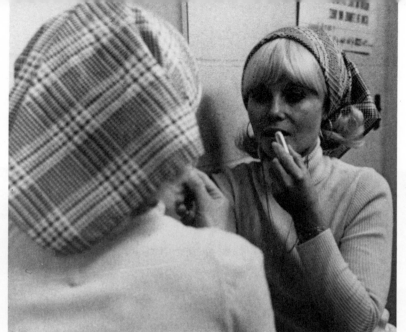

Makeup

Unlike most jockeys, Mary Bacon puts makeup on before going out on the track.

She rode Fifty Coins in this 1973 race at New York's Aqueduct and came in fourth.

Her "makeup" was more of a mudpack after she splashed down the stretch behind the leaders in a Monmouth Park race in 1974. Her mount, John's Patrol, finished fifth.

EIGHTIES

Young college football stars graduate and immediately excite the pro ranks: Doug Flutie . . . Dan Marino . . .

Veterans make their mark: Payton . . . Riggins . . .

On the ice: Islanders and Oilers . . . Torvil and Dean . . . the U.S. Olympic hockey team . . .

On the courts: Connors and McEnroe, Navratilova, King and Lloyd.

Mary Lou.

And Pete Rose.

This Beats the Band

There were four seconds remaining and Stanford was ahead of California, 20–19, in their game at Berkeley in November 1982. But Cal was to receive the kickoff; they planned to keep lateraling the ball back to a teammate to keep the return going.

In the confusion that followed, the ball went from Kevin Moen to Richard Rodgers, the special teams' captain, to Dwight Garner, back to Rodgers, to Marriet Ford, and then to Moen again.

Somewhere along the way, nearly everyone thought the play was over. Stanford substitutes came out on the field and so did both bands, from each end zone.

But Moen kept going, ran over a Stanford trombone player, and scored the winning touchdown in one of the most bizarre finishes to a game in college football history.

Cinderella On Ice

It was a storybook victory.

The U.S. hockey team had not been considered a strong contender for any medal at all at the 1980 Olympic Games at Lake Placid, New York.

But they stunned the world with come-from-behind wins, toppled the Soviet Union, a team that had not lost a game in Olympic competition in a dozen years, then beat Finland to assure the gold.

Goalie Jim Craig, draped in the American flag, personified the national pride in the triumph.

Drive and Dive

Golfer Jerry Pate approached the 18th green during the final round of the Western Open in Oak Brook, Illinois, in 1981—wearing a swim mask.

The previous week, Pate had celebrated his victory in the Memphis Classic by diving into a nearby pond.

Master-ful Dance

Bernhard Langer tried a little body English (or is it body German?), but he missed this putt on the 15th green at the Augusta National Golf Club, in Georgia.

He still won the tournament and claimed the 1985 Masters golf title.

Fatal Crash

The race car of Texas driver Gordon Smiley flew through the air and broke up after hitting a wall on a turn during a warm-up lap for qualification at the Indianapolis 500 in 1982.

Smiley was killed instantly.

Stop, Thief

Rickey Henderson, then of the Oakland A's, showed his grace and style and speed in stealing yet another base, this one against the Cleveland Indians in August 1982.

Henderson broke Lou Brock's single-season stolen-base record later that month, with number 130.

Doing the Valenzuela

It's not a dance; it's a windup.

Pitcher Fernando Valenzuela balanced on one leg and looked skyward when he pitched. Whatever, it worked.

The young pitching sensation of the Los Angeles Dodgers was Rookie of the Year in 1981 when he was just 21 years old. A 10-piece mariachi band showed up to help the Mexican-born pitcher celebrate. He was 13–7 that year, with a 2.46 earned run average—and he hit for a .250 average.

For an encore, Valenzuela set a major league record at the start of the 1985 season, going 41⅓ innings without allowing an earned run.

179

Hit Batter

Baltimore Orioles batter Dan Ford buckled and went down after being hit in the head by a pitch in the fifth inning of the second game of the 1983 World Series against the Philadelphia Phillies.

Ford was able to stay in the game after being hit by the pitch thrown by Charles Hudson of the Phillies.

Fair or Foul?

New York Yankees third baseman Graig Nettles and catcher Rick Cerone watched as a bunt off the bat of Kansas City Royals Frank White edged the third base line in the third inning of the second game of the 1980 American League playoffs.

It went foul.

Smash Hit

The bat shattered, but Philadelphia Phillies slugger Mike Schmidt still got a single in the fourth inning of Game 4 of the 1983 World Series against the Baltimore Orioles. His hit moved Pete Rose to third and set up a Phillies score.

Catcher Rick Dempsey and umpire Frank Pulli looked on.

Crash Course

The irresistible force is Los Angeles Dodger runner Dusty Baker. The immovable object is Montreal Expos catcher Gary Carter.

In this case, the immovable object won.

Carter held on to the ball as Baker tried to score on a single in the sixth inning of Game 4 of the 1981 National League playoffs.

Keeping an eye on things was umpire Dutch Rennert.

Classy Chris

Chris Evert became the dominant woman player in the world following the retirement of Margaret Court Smith and Billie Jean King.

As a poised, fiercely determined 20-year-old, Chris won her first U.S. ladies championship in 1975.

Chris (now Evert Lloyd) had won at least one of the four titles that constitute the Grand Slam every year since 1973 and had more than 1,000 career match victories, the winningest record in modern tennis history. The record included six U.S. Opens, six French Opens, three Wimbledons and two Australian Opens.

Marvelous Martina

A native of Czechoslovakia who became a U.S. citizen in 1981, Martina Navratilova dominated women's tennis in the 1980s.

The talented, powerful left-hander has an all-court game and her top world ranking, her record winning streak and six straight Grand Slam titles begs the question: Will she go down in history as the greatest women's tennis player ever?

She had her own answer:

"It's a very long term goal. And it's also a very subjective goal . . .

If you go on titles alone, then Margaret Court was the greatest. If you go on." Wimbledon titles, then Suzanne Lenglen or Helen Wills Moody were the greatest. If you go on longevity, then Chris (Evert Lloyd) would be the greatest, and perhaps I would be right behind her.

"So, it depends on what criteria you use. If you go on the best percentage over a certain period of time, then I'm right there because I've been playing so many matches and losing once or twice a year."

Year . . . after year . . . after year.

'Jimbo'

Jimmy Connors was considered the world's best men's tennis player in the mid-1970s—and one of the game's "bad boy" mavericks.

With a mercurial court temperament (some called it arrogant), he won five U.S. Open championships and two Wimbledon singles titles among numerous other top-flight matches.

Ranked among the top three world players in the '80s—and into his 30s—Connors provided memorable, often sensational, competition with the likes of rivals John McEnroe, Bjorn Borg and Ivan Lendl.

188

It was only practice on the first day of qualifications for the 1983 Indianapolis 500, but veteran driver Dick Simon of San Juan Capistrano, California, already was in hot water.

Fire broke out in the rear of his racing car. Simon was able to get out of the tight cockpit quickly and was not injured.

The Brat or the Best?

The Brat or the Best? John McEnroe may have been both at one time or another.

At the U.S. Pro Indoor Championships in Philadelphia in 1975, he pushed a television cameraman and his camera that he felt were too close to him. Then, McEnroe went on to win the tourney for the fourth straight year.

His temper was, for a time, as famous as his textbook tennis. His belligerent behavior had been chastized by the British press and had earned him frequent fines from tennis officialdom.

In cooler reflection, he was able to boast four Wimbledon singles titles, a Grand Prix tennis point total record, and four U.S. Open championships.

And still counting.

Considered the top men's player in the world in 1983 and again in 1984, he was increasingly compared with the best players the game has known.

Running's a Drag

It was the first-ever Olympic women's marathon, and it turned out to be a heart-wrenching one.

Gaby Andersen-Scheiss, a 39-year-old Sun Valley, Idaho, teacher who was representing Switzerland, did just fine for the first 25 miles of the race and was among the leaders. But exhaustion and dehydration caught up with her as she entered the Los Angeles Memorial Coliseum for the last laps of the historic 1984 Olympic race.

"The worst part was when I got into the Coliseum," she said later. "It was a lot hotter."

She staggered, meandered, wobbled—but would not give up. Millions watched her at the Coliseum and on television screens worldwide and pulled for her to finish. Medical attendants followed her along the last lap. So did her husband.

If she were touched by any of them before the finish, she would be disqualified.

As she crossed the finish line, with classic determination, she collapsed into the arms of attendants.

A First

The race belonged to Joan Benoit. Virtually from start to finish.

The courageous runner took the lead at about the 2½-mile mark in the first-ever Olympic women's marathon in 1984 and was never challenged. She won the gold with a time of 2 hours 24 minutes 52 seconds for the 26-mile, 385-yard endurance test.

Just 17 days before the Olympic trials, the Freeport, Maine, runner had arthroscopic knee surgery. But she ran, in pain, and qualified, winning the trials easily. She did the same in the Olympics.

She later said she wasn't bothered by the smoggy Los Angeles air during the race and added that she never really felt threatened by her competition.

"I followed the yellow brick road, so to speak. I said to myself, 'You feel too good to blow this one.' "

Greta Waitz of Norway, the 1983 world champion, finished second in 2:26:18, followed by Rosa Mota of Portugal in 2:26:57.

Pixie Perfect

She's a gymnast with a tomboyish, exuberant style, who loves to play to the crowds, a 4-foot 9-inch teen-ager from West Virginia with a winning smile and a winning style.

At the age of 16, Mary Lou Retton, of Fairmont, West Virginia, was America's greatest female gymnast—perhaps, at the time, the world's.

Surely, it seemed so from her performance at the Summer Olympics in Los Angeles in 1984. She launched herself into a twisting, tumbling perfect-10 vault on her final exercise, adding it to another perfect score on floor exercises, to capture the all-around women's gymnastics title and give the United States its first-ever Olympic gold medal in the event.

She already had led the U.S. squad to a silver medel behind Romania in the team finals and had won the hearts and admiration of all who had seen her breathtaking acrobatics and spunky personality.

Indy Wreck

Driver Danny Ongais, a former drag racing champion, was among the leaders in the 64th lap of the 1981 Indianapolis 500 when his car suddenly veered to the right on a turn and slammed into the outer wall.

Tires flew everywhere; metal exploded all over. Flames enveloped what was left of the car.

Ongais was hospitalized with multiple injuries. The fiery crash caused one of 11 yellow cautions, which slowed the race considerably for 69 of the 200 laps. Mario Andretti was declared the winner, even though he crossed the finish behind Bobby Unser, who was penalized a lap for passing cars under a yellow caution flag on the 149th lap.

Ongais wasn't long out of the driver's seat, however.

He came back to team with Ted Field in 1982 to win two straight at Daytona International Speedway.

Decker on the Deck

Mary Decker's dream of an Olympic gold medal turned into a nightmare of frustration when the American favorite collided with Zola Budd midway during the 3,000-meter run in Los Angeles in 1984.

Romania's Maricica Puica won the gold, Britain's Wendy Sly the silver, and Lynn Williams of Canada the bronze, but the finish order was overshadowed by the controversy of the mid-race tumult.

Dan Marino

Small steps backward for a man, but a giant record for a quarterback.

Miami Dolphins QB Dan Marino fades back to pass during the first half of a December 1984 game against the Dallas Cowboys. In this last regular-season game of the year, Marino broke the season record for most yards gained, passing. That same year, he also set the mark for most TD passes.

In Super Bowl XIX in January 1985 against the San Francisco 49ers, Marino watches as a pass goes incomplete. The 'Niners won, 38–16.

Style He Has . . .

It's the ball he doesn't have.

In a preseason game in March 1984, outfielder Rickey Henderson fell back in a fruitless effort to catch a high fly off the bat of Milwaukee Brewer Charlie Moore.

The ball can be seen at the "T" in Style.

Henderson's uniform, incidentally, was soon out of style. He was traded from the Oakland A's to the New York Yankees.

Riggo

On the field, he breathed fire. But sometimes football running back John Riggins needed a little oxygen to keep the fire burning while on the sidelines.

The Washington Redskins runner took some oxygen during the first half of Super Bowl XVII against the Miami Dolphins— a game in which he rushed for a record 166 yards. That was at age 33 and in his 11th season.

Sweetness

Records didn't mean much when Walter "Sweetness" Payton had the ball.

O. J. Simpson's single-game record of 273 was topped by Payton's 275 in 1977.

He took the career yardage record from the great Jim Brown in 1984.

To Payton, it was the chase that made it fun.

"It motivates me, keeps me going," the Chicago Bear running back once said. "But once you have it, it loses its glitter."

Records or no, Walter Payton will never lose his glitter.

Hand to Mouth

Cleveland Cavalier defender Roy
Hinson slapped his hand over the
mouth of Boston Celtics center Robert
Parish during a scramble under the
basket in a 1985 playoff game.
 The Celtics won the playoff series.

Dr. J

Graceful and talented, one of the most
dazzling players ever on the
basketball court, Julius Erving, "Dr. J,"
is one of the best and most popular
superstars.
 He started out with the New York
Nets of the old American Basketball
Association and earned his superstar
credentials with the Philadelphia
'76ers.
 A seven-time NBA All-Star (he
joined the league in 1977) with a
career scoring average of better than
23 points a game, Erving has been
described as one of the few players
who can ignite a crowd and
demoralize an opponent with one
move.

Call to Arms

Two of the greats of professional basketball in an uncharacteristic pose: Philadelphia '76er Julius Erving and Boston Celtic Larry Bird in a scuffle during a Boston Garden game in 1984.

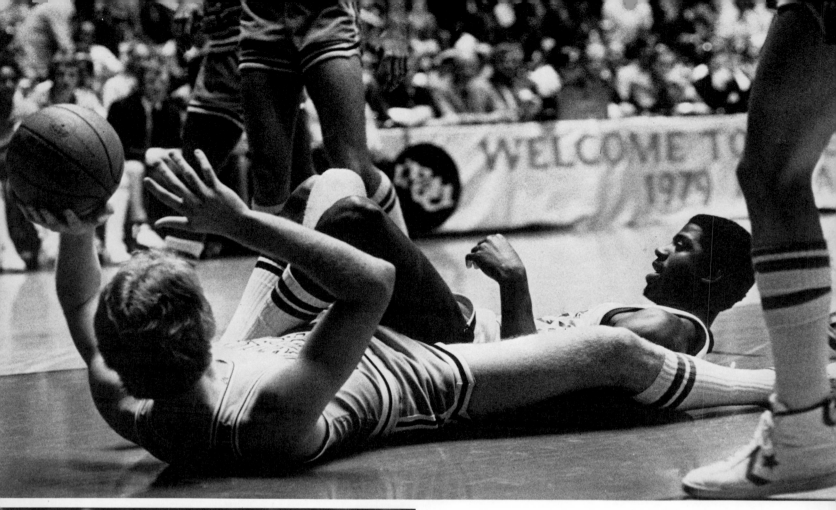

The Basketball Bird

Larry Bird, the hometown hero of French Lick, Indiana, probably is the most complete player in pro basketball: a shooter, a passer, a playmaker, and the heart and soul of the Boston Celtics of the 1980s.

In 1979–80, Bird was Rookie of the Year. In 1981, when the Celtics won their 14th championship, Bird was the Most Valuable Player in the playoffs.

His teammates stress his ability to go 100 percent, day in and day out, always enthusiastic, always hustling.

He's played against some of the best since his college days at Indiana State. In this 1979 photo, Bird was on his back to toss the ball to a teammate during a scramble with Earvin "Magic" Johnson of UCLA in the NCAA championship game.

In the pros, perhaps his toughest opposition has been Julius Erving of the '76ers.

Miami 'Miracle'

They call it a "Hail Mary," as it's virtually a prayer. Usually it goes unanswered.

But with the last seconds ticking off and Boston College behind Miami, 45–40, in the 1984 Orange Bowl, BC quarterback Doug Flutie threw it up there for grabs.

Wide receiver Gerard Phelan (No. 20) somehow got behind all the defenders in the end zone, including Reggie Sutton (No. 1), who leapt high to block it. Phelan hauled it in.

The dramatic finish gave Boston College a 47–45 win.

The King Is Dead . . . Long Live the King

The coveted Stanley Cup was held high by a jubilant Wayne Gretzky as the Edmonton Oilers celebrated their first National Hockey League Championship, in May 1984.

The Oilers won the Cup in five games over the New York Islanders, who had won four straight championships, including a four-game sweep of the Oilers the previous year.

Gretzky, who held 35 league scoring records, led the Oilers to a repeat championship in 1985—setting playoff records with 17 goals, 30 assists and 47 points.

"We wanted to show people we are not a flash in the pan," said the 24-year-old center after the second championship.

"We wanted the second one more than the first and we worked extremely hard to get it."

Boss(y) of the Ice

Mike Bossy of the New York Islanders holds the coveted
Stanley Cup aloft for all to admire as his teammates surround
him after the final victory over the Vancouver Canucks in
1982.

Bossy scored two goals and was voted Most Valuable
Player in the playoffs.

For a while, it seemed as though the Islanders owned the
Cup. They won four titles in a row before giving it up to the
Edmonton Oilers.

Follow the Bouncing Puck

Goalie Pelle Lindbergh of the Philadelphia Flyers has his eyes peeled to the puck as it bounces around in a 1985 game against the New York Islanders.

Lindbergh helped the Flyers eliminate the Islanders in the Patrick Division championship.

A Perfect Kiss

It almost melted the ice at the Sarajevo Olympics in 1984.

Jayne Torvil and Christopher Dean kissed during a sensational performance in ice dancing. The British team racked up an unprecedented 12 perfect scores to win the gold for the performance—and the hearts of spectators around the world.

Something Big

Patrick Ewing, the 7-foot center from Georgetown University, was the most widely hailed college player since Kareem Abdul-Jabbar was Lew Alcindor.

A three-time All-American, the Jamaican-born Ewing led Georgetown to the national collegiate championship game in three of his four years, topped by an NCAA title in 1984.

Ewing, who also played on the 1984 U.S. Olympic basketball team, is a dominating player and a fierce defender.

He was the big prize for the professional New York Knicks, who were able to make him their No. 1 draft pick after a seven-team lottery drawing for the privilege.

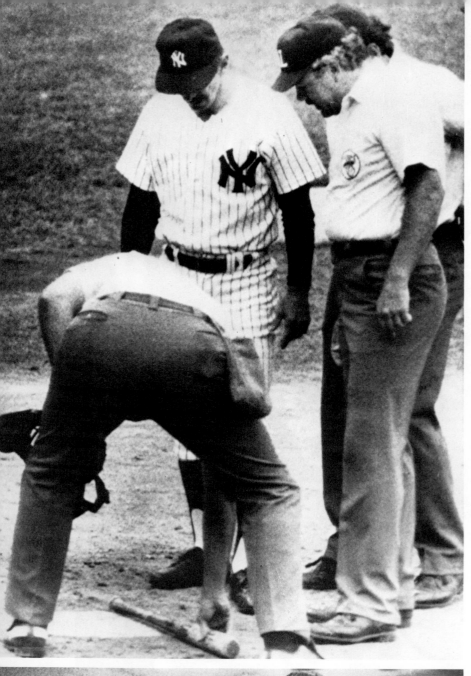

Tale of the Lonesome Pine

It was 34½ inches long and weighed 32 ounces, much like many other major league baseball bats.

What made this one unique, at least according to a crew of umpires, was an excessive amount of pine tar. The rules say pine tar, used by many players for a better grip, cannot be more than 18 inches up the bat handle.

After Kansas City Royals slugger George Brett hit a two-run homer off New York Yankee reliever "Goose" Gossage in the ninth inning of a game in July 1983, the Yankees protested. Umpire Tim McClelland used the plate to measure the pine tar on the handle as Yankee manager Billy Martin and umpire Joe Brinkman watched.

After a long discussion, the home run was disallowed, the score reverted to 4–3 in the Yankees' favor—and out stormed Brett. To no avail; the umpires' decision held.

But, an appeal made to American League president Lee MacPhail allowed Brett's homer to stand. MacPhail ordered the game completed (in August)—and Kansas City won.

Fowl Play

The Chicken is out at the plate with Philadelphia Phillies catcher Ozzie Virgil between innings of a 1985 game with the Houston Astros in the Astrodome.

Thrill . . . and Agony

New Zealand's Rod Dixon is obviously thrilled with his victory in the 1983 New York City Marathon.

But behind him, Britain's Geoff Smith collapsed just over the finish line.

Smith was passed by Dixon with just about one-quarter of a mile to go in the grueling race.

Just months before, Dixon had won the 7.4-mile Bay to Breakers race in San Francisco, for the second straight year.

'Charlie Hustle'

"Charlie Hustle" they call him.

Pete Rose is one of those players who goes all out in every game, running out every batted ball, sliding head first into a base, leaping for a line drive.

He became the first player in the National League to reach 4,000 hits—and he did it 21 years to the day after he got his first major league hit, a triple.

When Rose broke in with the Cincinnati Reds in 1963, he was named Rookie of the Year. His honors since have included National League Most Valuable Player in 1973 and MVP of the 1975 World Series.

He also holds the record for the most lifetime singles.

The feisty Rose played 16 years with the Reds before signing as a free agent with the Philadelphia Phillies. He helped the Phillies win the 1980 World Series, and later signed with the Montreal Expos.

Ironically, Rose got his 4,000th hit against his former team, the Reds, in April 1984. Here, he watches the ball as he heads for first on the double off Jerry Koosman.

In late 1984, at the age of 43, when he was second only to the great Ty Cobb in lifetime hits, he returned to Cincinnati as player-manager.